P9-BZH-808

Contents

Note to the Reader

The Real Estate Game is written in the masculine gender. Nothing is meant by the exclusive use of "he," "him" and "his." The real estate game, although in my opinion sexy, is asexual in that it can be played equally well by women and men. In fact, as the only barriers to entry and hurdles to success are *one's own* knowledge, desire and creativity, the real estate game is a great avenue for personal expression and growth—without sexual restrictions or bias.

The
Real Estate
Game

The
Real Estate
Game ─────────
And How To Win It

by
Jim Randel

Facts On File Publications
New York, New York ● Oxford, England

The Real Estate Game
And How To Win It

Copyright © 1986, 1987 by Jim Randel

Library of Congress Cataloging-in-Publication Data

Randel, Jim.
  The real estate game, and how to win it.

  Includes index.
  1. Real estate business. 2. Real estate investment.
I. Title.
HD1379.R37 1986   332.63'24   85-25277
ISBN 0-8160-1693-3 (HC)
ISBN 0-8160-1312-8 (PB)

Printed in United States of America

10 9 8 7 6 5 4 3 2

Composition by Facts On File/Circle Graphics

To Carol,
who puts everything in perspective.

Acknowledgments

I hope that in reading this book you'll feel my sense of excitement with the real estate game. That excitement derives not only from my own involvement in the game but also from an association with many players/entrepreneurs whose passion is contagious. I thank these people for sharing their ups (and, at times, downs) with me.

I'd also like to thank the following more sedate (but also exhilarating) friends: Bob Connolly, for extending me my first loan and for having an open mind and a creative spirit; John Dougherty, for his advice on the present and proposed tax laws; Josh Gaspero and Mike Morris for believing in this book; and Kate Kelly for her excellent editorial comments and counsel.

Introduction

"Ninety percent of all millionaires became so through owning real estate. More money has been made in real estate than in all industrial investments combined."

Andrew Carnegie

Whether or not Mr. Carnegie's numerical estimate is exact, in my opinion, his premise is indisputable: real estate[1] is far and away the road most often traveled to self-made wealth. This book is about that road—how to get on it, how to travel it.

This book is written as an introduction, addressed to anyone with an interest in real estate. It does not assume prior knowledge, education or experience. It presumes only a willingness to learn and a strong determination to better your situation. The key is desire, for, in my judgment, success with real estate is more a function of diligence, creativity and perseverance than unusual intelligence or extensive education.

The intent of the book is to open your mind to the proposition that you can achieve financial independence with real estate. Thousands of people have, many starting with little (or no) capital and no special education or experience. And thousands more will do so in the future; perhaps you will be one of them.

This book describes a specific program designed to achieve real estate wealth, an approach I call the "real estate game." Participants in the game are "players" who "score" with a successful deal.

The real estate game is not the exclusive route to real estate *wealth*. However, I believe that it is the style of "investment"[2] used by the great majority of real estate's self-made millionaires. And it is without question the approach to real estate investment most likely to yield the maximum reward in the minimum time.

The real estate game is a style of acquiring, financing, leasing and/or selling real estate which is active, creative and ambitious. The real estate player, seeking quicker[3] returns far greater in amount than traditionally expected from real estate,[4] views real estate with a unique perspective. The real estate player sees a piece of real estate as an opportunity—as an asset to be *actively used* to turn little money into lots of money in short periods of time. While most real estate investors acquire real estate with the hope that inflation and other natural forces will increase its value (see chapter 2), the real estate player doesn't wait for outside forces—he attempts to make his property's value increase immediately.

The real estate game is not necessarily high risk. Some of the ideas described in this book involve considerable risk; most do not. What really makes the real estate game distinguishable is its viewpoint:

1. Look at each deal as a chance to double, triple, etc. your cash quickly; don't be satisfied with anything less.

2. Take an active, aggressive approach toward each deal; don't wait for inflation or other forces to increase value—*create value*.

3. *Use* your real estate as an asset to make money; don't stop with acquisition—explore all possible *post-closing* opportunities to make money.

The real estate game is not just a theory. There are thousands of players throughout the United States who are right now making money with real estate faster and in greater amounts than anything even hoped for by the average investor. This book aims to put you in that group.

The Real Estate Game, however, is not just about money, for there is another dimension to the real estate game—an excitement, a magic, an allure. Perhaps it is the magnitude and force of real estate, or its stability and substance, its visibility and glitter, the competitive interaction with other real estate players, the satisfaction of a successful project. Whatever the reasons, the fact is that you may well find the real estate game to be addictive.

Harry Helmsley, one of the wealthiest individuals in America,[5] and all self-made in real estate, speaks for many others when responding to a question about retirement:

> As long as I've got my health, I'll just keep right on going. I'm having so much fun, I don't know what I could do that would give me as much pleasure.[6]

Mr. Helmsley's endorsement should tell you something. Here is a man with the financial ability to do anything in the world he wants, yet he continues to "slug it out" in the real estate game—because it is *fun*. The fact is that Helmsley is only one of the hundreds of real estate players who, although having long ago gained financial independence, continue to play the game.

Any book which guarantees results is a hoax. I do, however, submit that it is extremely difficult to achieve independence/real wealth by earning a fixed income; after living expenses and taxes, there never seems to be enough left. And I can affirm that a large number of ordinary people have attained financial independence (and in many cases substantial wealth) by directing their time and energy into the real estate game.

I suggest that you think of your time and energy as capital—as an asset which can be invested to earn you a return. As with any asset, there are many ways to invest your own time and energy—some more rewarding than others. Although most people don't think of it as such, going to work every day and earning a salary is an investment decision, for it is a specific use of your time and energy. Since it, to some extent, precludes other uses, one must analyze and review this investment. Are you investing your most valuable asset—your own time and energy—in that endeavor most likely to lead to your financial goals? If not, I suggest that you give the real estate game a serious look.

First you must have a game plan. Chapter 1 describes ways to play the game, outlining different approaches being used successfully by real estate players across the country. It will give you some ideas about the best ways for you to play the game.

Chapters 2 through 8 describe the basics of the game: knowledge and information. The rules and concepts of the real estate game must of course, be learned before one attempts a deal, but they are not overly complicated and, once mastered, will stand you in good stead to try any deal, no matter what the size.

Chapter 9 speaks to the art of selling—in its broadest sense, the art of persuading others to act as you'd like them to. Needless to say, an ability to convince others to buy, to sell, to loan or to lease is a great plus for the real estate player.

Chapter 10 reviews entrepreneurship and its role in the real estate game. The premise is that playing the real estate game is entrepreneurial in nature and that the stronger your entrepreneurial instincts, the greater the commitment you may wish to make to the game. The chapter analyzes entrepreneurship in an attempt to help you identify the level of commitment to the game with which you're most comfortable.

Chapter 11 summarizes the book with some concluding thoughts which I call the Ten Keys to Success at the Real Estate Game.

One final note on reading this book. I have used notes throughout this book; these notes appear at the end of each chapter. These notes are meant as supplemental information to those interested and need not be read to understand the text.

The Real Estate Game aims to start you thinking about real estate and to suggest that your financial objectives are very attainable if you are willing to make a commitment to success. The real estate game has worked for many people; I hope that you will give it a try.

Notes to Introduction

1.   "Real estate": land and the improvements thereon.

2.   The real estate game—a *very active* involvement with the asset acquired—is quite different from most investments, in which the investor's role is passive once the investment decision is made.

3.   The real estate game might be called the microwave approach to real estate wealth.

4.   Or from any other type of investment.

5.   The 1984 *Forbes* 400 issue lists Mr. Helmsley as one of America's wealthiest individuals, with an estimated net worth of $900 million.

6.   Robert L. Shook, *The Real Estate People* (New York: Harper & Row, 1980).

1

Game Plans

There are a lot of different ways to make money in the real estate game. The approach you take should depend on:

1. the amount of time you have to commit to the game

2. the financial objectives you set for yourself

3. the time frame in which you'd like to achieve your financial objectives and

4. the amount of risk you are willing to accept.

This chapter discusses five different game plans, several of which overlap and each of which is being used successfully by many game players. The five selected plans are in no way exclusive. One of the great things about the real estate game is that there are innumerable ways to play it. The five plans are just suggestions—outlines you may wish to refer to in devising your own strategy.

Game Plan 1: Maximum Leverage— Then Ride with the Tide

The plan is to acquire as many properties as you can, using the principles of leverage and creative financing, and then enjoy the ride of inflation/appreciation. Because single-family houses or small multi-family buildings are generally easier to find and acquire than larger multi-family or commercial[1] properties, most Game Plan 1 players buy houses or multi-family buildings of, say, five units or less.

Our company started in the real estate game buying and renting single-family houses. Eventually, we moved into multi-family housing and then commercial properties. Many people start and stay with single-family houses[2] or small multi-family buildings.[3]

Getting familiar with one geographical area (usually a town, city or county), Game Plan 1 players eventually become expert in spotting and acquiring good values. They learn the rental market and know on sight what a home or apartment should rent for. They establish a relationship with one or two lenders—which usually isn't too difficult, as most savings banks and savings-and-loan associations are very comfortable loaning against single-family houses or small multi-family buildings. The brokers in the area soon learn what these players are looking for and begin calling them first whenever the right property becomes available. Soon the players are well positioned to acquire two to three rental houses or small multi-family buildings per year.

The Game Plan 1 players generally finance quite aggressively in that they spread their capital as far as possible and acquire as many properties as they can. Their logic is to maximize the return on their money by spreading it into as much real estate as possible, then benefiting in multiples as inflation increases value.[4] Notwithstanding this aggressive financing, I believe that Plan 1, if well executed,[5] involves limited risk for several reasons: First, people always need housing. So long as the properties are reasonably well located and fairly standard[6] in size and livability, there should be a steady stream of potential tenants.[7] Second, these properties are usually very marketable. Therefore, if a player needs or desires to liquidate his equity by selling,[8] there is almost always a demand for these types of properties.[9]

Although the returns from Game Plan 1 are tied to inflation and thus arguably limited,[10] if you are able to acquire just one or two properties a year (and get them to or near breakeven),[11] after just three or four years you will find that you have built up quite a nice net worth, which will increase dramatically every year. The reasons are quite simple: if you buy property with 5% down and the inflation rate is 5%, *then you will at least double your original investment every year.* The key is leverage, for inflation increases the value of 100% of your asset, even though 95% of it was acquired with somebody else's (that is, borrowed) money.

Game Plan 1 is a good, steady approach to the game. It is not time consuming and doesn't require that you leave your present job. Compared to earning a salary, it's a great way to accumulate wealth, and once you've got the system down, you will find that acquiring a property or two a year is not that difficult. What often happens, however, is that Game Plan 1 players—experiencing how lucrative and enjoyable the real estate game can be—begin to look for ways to increase[12] and accelerate their returns. Sooner or later, most of them venture into one of the other game plans, where the objective is to *create value* and earn returns far in excess of anything tied to inflation or any other traditional economic force.

Game Plan 2: Renovation

Game Plans 2, 3, 4 and 5 involve the creation of value through post-closing activity. Unlike the game players using Plan 1, who buy and then let inflation take over, game players using Plans 2, 3, 4 and 5 view acquisition as only the first step.

In these game plans, the risk may be higher than in Game Plan 1, but so is the potential upside and the speed with which financial objectives can be met. The essence of all of these plans is the act(s) of *doing something* to real estate which increases its worth—that is, *creates value.*

Game Plan 2 involves renovation—the physical alteration of a building. Renovation can run the gamut from repainting to extensive structural changes. The objective is to create value in multiples of the cost of the renovation.

In 1977 I started buying single-family houses. My objective was to buy property which was undervalued[13] because of easily correctable reasons—problems which could be overcome without major renovation.[14] I would then buy[15] and renovate, the general approach being to try to limit renovation to cosmetics.[16] Once the property was renovated, I would either resell or refinance, hoping to overfinance based on the new value. The key was to do renovations which would cost $X but would add value at least four to five times $X.

As an example, my first purchase was a house bought for $60,000. The house had been lived in for many years by an elderly man and showed very poorly—it appeared dark and dirty—even though it was basically a very nice house. The building inspection revealed no structural problems and a contractor friend estimated that the cosmetic changes which I wanted to make would cost $10,000.

I asked a lawyer friend to introduce me to a senior officer in a good local bank and I went to see this person. He indicated a willingness to loan me $60,000 to buy the house on a one-year "construction" loan but only if I could get someone with a good financial statement[17] to cosign the loan. I was in town just a couple of months and didn't really know anybody whom I could ask to cosign, but a friend of mine knew someone and thus my friend became my partner,[18] his job being to bring in the individual with the strong credit to cosign the loan. My partner's credit contact cosigned as a favor, after we convinced him that there was minimal risk and that he'd be off the loan within three months.

We now had the $60,000 to buy, but we still needed $10,000 for the renovation. I went to a local commercial bank to obtain a loan but could get only $5,000 and for just 90 days. I took it and then went to see my contractor friend and asked him whether he'd do the $10,000 worth of work—with $5,000 down and the balance in three months. I offered him an extra $1,000 if he would wait for the second $5,000. He agreed.

The day we closed we immediately started renovation, for we were under a tight time schedule:

- one-year construction loan

- 90-day $5,000 loan
- 90-day obligation to contractor
- promise to cosigner to get him off the loan within 90 days and
- interest running on the $60,000[19] and $5,000 loans and no money to make the payments.

The objective of the renovation was to change the look and feel of the house—to open it up and "show off" its good features. The work was cosmetic: painting, sanding and staining the wood floors, new bathroom fixtures, rebuilding a porch/deck.

While the renovation was under way, I lined up a few brokers to appraise the finished house. The day the renovations were done, the house was advertised for rent and the brokers were brought in to do their evaluations. My partner and I anxiously waited for their numbers.

The three valuations were in the $110,000 range and we breathed a sigh of relief. I asked the brokers to put their appraisals in writing (one paragraph), took them to the bank and asked for a permanent mortgage, based on the brokers' valuation.[20] Based on my new value, the bank offered me a permanent loan of $80,000, at a fixed interest rate of 9% (the going rate at that time), with monthly payments of about $650. As the bank was comfortable with the equity in the house ($30,000), they did not require a cosignature. So, we immediately refinanced (within 90 days) and used the additional $20,000 (the amount over the $60,000 construction mortgage which we repaid) to:

- pay the interest due on the $60,000 loan
- repay the $5,000 commercial loan plus interest
- pay the contractor $6,000 and
- buy the cosigner a gift.[21]

We still had about $8,000 left, $2,000 of which we put in the bank to cover debt service and taxes until we could rent the house. The balance ($6,000) we divided up, each of us putting $3,000 (nontaxable[22]) money in our pockets. As the house now showed very nicely, we soon located a tenant willing to pay $750/month plus utilities, which covered our debt service, real estate taxes and insurance.

As a result of this deal, my partner and I:

- each made $3,000 (after taxes)
- controlled an asset worth $110,000, giving us total equity of $30,000, which asset was appreciating
- were receiving depreciation which sheltered other income (we were both starting out as lawyers)
- were repaying the $80,000 mortgage with someone else's money, that is, the tenant's payments (rent) were being used to make the mortgage payments and we were building equity by paying down the mortgage
- had established credibility with the local brokerage community
- had established credit with a local contractor and
- had established credit with a lending institution.

Not only had we laid the framework to do more and bigger deals, but—counting the equity in the house—we each made $18,000 ($36,000 total) in 90 days on an investment of zero. Needless to say, this deal whet our appetite for more of the same.

In subsequent years, what became a real estate company acquired and renovated several commercial properties, using the same principles as described here. The effort was always the same: to create value through renovation by changing the appearance of a property. The technique has worked for us—and many others—time and again.

Game Plan 3: Finding Your Niche

One of the ways to create value in real estate is to approach it in a way most other people can't. In other words, identify a niche with regard to some use or application of real estate and become expert at it.

The best way to make money in business is to do something which nobody else can do. Because this is an ideal (since sooner or later others will fill the vacuum), the next best thing is to be in a position to do something which few others can do. This theory can be applied to the real estate game.

Some real estate players have made a business of attempting "to score" single-family houses—find the grossly underpriced house, buy it and then resell it. The problem with this approach is that it is very difficult to find such houses for two reasons: (1) there are *lots* of other people around who can value a single-family house and (2) since house sales are a *common* transaction, most sellers have a good information base on which to value their house. Conversely, if you can approach the real estate game in a way that *few* others do or can, your chances of scoring on a deal are greatly increased.

There are several examples of Game Plan 3:

New Construction/Development

Not many people can look at a piece of commercial land and tell you what it's worth. Those who can are real estate developers and/or builders. They know the zoning in the area, the value of the location, the hard costs of construction, the soft costs of development, the ways to finance new construction, the ways to finance the finished project and the rentability (marketability) of the completed product. With this specialized knowledge, they can evaluate land and sometimes acquire real bargains, for *few* others have the ability to similarly evaluate land and bid against them. They can also use their unique knowledge (and abilities) to create value in the land—to apply what they know—and turn the land into a money-making venture. Not many people know how to do that; that is one reason that real estate builders/developers do so well.[23]

One obviously cannot approach a large-scale development without years of experience and considerable backing. But attempting a small-scale new construction project is not out of the question, even for a beginning real estate player.

If, for example, you can obtain an option on a piece of land,[24] you can use the lead time to:

1. retain a good attorney and determine what zoning and other approvals are necessary to build on the land

2. obtain zoning and all other required approvals

3. speak with architects regarding the size and design of a building on the land

4. speak with contractors regarding cost and time estimates for constructing the building designed by the architect

5. speak with lenders regarding financing the construction and permanent phases of the development

6. estimate the soft costs of the development, including (after you get a time estimate from the contractor and an interest rate estimate from the lender) construction interest

7. speak with brokers regarding the marketability of/ demand for the finished space and at what price

8. speak with prospective tenants, showing them renderings of the proposed building[25] and

9. analyze the numbers to determine whether the deal, taking into account a risk factor and potential profit, makes sense.

All of these items are "learnable" within a relatively short period of time. If you are willing to spend the time (and some money) to work with an attorney, architect, builder and lender, you can learn a lot and perhaps put yourself in a position to do a new construction project.

I am not suggesting that once you have the knowledge, success is guaranteed. Needless to say, you still have to locate a good piece of land and then perform: get your approvals, get the project financed, get the building built (within the budget), get the building leased (at the projected rentals).[26] But, I am suggesting that with the right knowledge and energy you can position yourself to make money on real estate the way few others can—essentially, giving yourself the opportunity to score by doing something that few others can. And the financial rewards of a successful development will be commensurate with your unique knowledge and ability.

Find Yourself a Tenant

Another way to create a niche for yourself is to establish a relationship with one or more national tenants and to work to find them suitable locations. If the tenant has good credit, you can tie up property with the knowledge and confidence that it will be financeable (given the lease with "your" tenant) and, of course, rented.

As an example, perhaps you are able to establish a good relationship with one of the fast-food companies like Burger King. You spend time with them and learn exactly what they require by way of a prospective location. You may learn that they wish to build and own their own buildings, but that they will ground-lease land at $X/square foot. You learn their demographic and site requirements. They assure you that if you find the right piece of land they will give you a quick decision.

With this data, you can go to the street and start talking to owners and brokers. Unless Burger King has already called all the brokers in the area (doubtful), you have unique information which you can use to your advantage. You may, for example, find an owner who has no idea what to do with his land and absolutely no inkling that Burger King might be interested. Accordingly, you may be able to acquire the land[27] at a price with which the owner is quite satisfied but which (given the lease in your pocket) is also a very favorable price for you. You then turn around and lease the land (sometimes called a "ground lease") to Burger King, at a rental which presumably gives you a very nice profit.[28] What you have done essentially is use information—which few other people have—to "create value" in the land by leasing it to a tenant whose interest nobody else was aware of.

Many developers are successful today because of their relationships with national tenants.[29] For example, a strip shopping center developer who knows he has an "anchor" tenant[30] interested in leasing at a particular location can acquire land that other people might be reluctant to buy on speculation. And since only the developer knows about this anchor tenant, the price of the land will reflect the limited demand.

Establishing a relationship with a national tenant—while not easy for the beginning real estate player—is nevertheless possible. Needless to say, the big department stores will not be available to you but the smaller fast-food, supermarket or pharmacy-type users may be. It is in their interest to find new locations and thus most of them will be happy to explain to you their site requirements. If, over time, you can develop a good relationship with one of these companies, you will have created something very valuable in that you can use your tenant over and over again as a tool to help you acquire and lease property.

Becoming an Expert

Some players develop an expertise in either a particular geographical area or a particular aspect of development, such as zoning. With their unique knowledge, they are able to identify or create deals that others cannot see or do.

As an example, I know an individual who has limited his game playing to a very defined underdeveloped area. He knows everything going on in the area and quite simply has a more extensive and up-to-date information base than anyone else who owns, sells, buys or rents in this area. He is constantly using this information to his advantage, buying properties at great prices and locating tenants that others didn't even know were looking in the area. Quite simply, he has made himself an expert who creates value by being more knowledgeable than his competition (sellers, other buyers and other landlords). The result is that he does at least one or two very good deals each year.

Similarly, someone who develops an expertise in a facet of development such as zoning can more correctly and quickly evaluate commercial land than can his competition. If he uses this expertise properly, he should be able to find and acquire underpriced property, by knowing things that most others don't know and thus separating himself from the crowd.

The gist of Game Plan 3 is to separate yourself from the pack. To use a relationship, information, or knowledge to your competitive advantage. It's a great way to succeed in the real estate game, for the development of relationships or the acquisition of information or knowledge is attainable without financial investment. The beginning real estate player who is long on energy and desire but short on money can use his time and energy to learn—to read, to talk with others, to observe. With a unique relationship, key information or specialized knowledge, he can find financial backers and parlay his "assets" into a real estate deal, in which he will be positioned to use his assets to create value for himself and his partners.

Game Plan 4: Creating an Illusion

Real estate value, as with beauty, is in the eyes of the beholder. Real estate has no absolute value—its worth is what a buyer will pay to own it, a tenant will pay to rent it or a lender will loan against it. The objective of Game Plan 4 is to effect a change in how people perceive a piece of real estate, in other words, to create an illusion that the old property is gone and a new—much more valuable—property has taken its place.

The illusion can be created in one or more of several ways: renovation and physical improvement, change in usage, new leasing program, public relations and management, etc. The objective is to convince the world that they are viewing a property so radically changed from the way it existed before as to constitute a whole new property. If you are successful in creating this illusion you may really score, given that you bought the "old" property at one value and are now selling, renting or financing a "new" property—at an entirely different set of values. And the "new" value may be a tremendous multiple[31] of the cost of the transition. What's more, the transition can occur in a relatively short period of time.

Following are three examples of Game Plan 4:

Where's the Old Apartment Building?

Both with small and large apartment properties, an owner can attempt to change the stature of the property in an effort to attract higher-paying tenants. Throughout the United States there are apartment buildings which have been allowed to run down—in terms of appearance, maintenance and/or management. The world sees an old (the property may not even be that old in terms of years), worn down, poorly run building and only "low-rent" tenants will occupy the apartments. Accordingly, the rent roll is low and, consequently, the property's value.

This property may be ideal for the real estate player using Game Plan 4. He will acquire this property *at its present value* (based on its current rent roll) and then through a process of physical improvement, higher leasing standards, better maintenance and management and public relations go about altering its image.[32] The desired result is a whole new group of tenants, a whole new rent roll *and* a new value. If the player has spent his transition money wisely, the financial result of this effort may be a real home run in terms of cash flow, value and/or financeability. And (in contrast to Game Plan 1) the financial reward may come very quickly, for the player has *created* instant value instead of waiting for appreciation to happen.

Upgrading

Through a process similar to that described above, many players buy older office buildings or shopping centers and attempt to upgrade the building's image. For example, in many parts of Manhattan, good real estate players are buying office buildings the rent rolls of which reflect rates far below the current market. Then, through a process which includes among other things:

1. the buy-out of older, under-market tenants

2. a new leasing program seeking more prestigious, higher-paying tenants

3. new amenities, such as high-speed elevators

4. cosmetics, such as redecorating the lobby

5. renovation, such as an improved HVAC system

6. new and improved management and

7. extensive public relations and advertising campaign,

these players attempt to create a "brand new" building. Once again, the game plan is to create the illusion that a "new" building has taken the place of the old—to convince prospective tenants, lenders and/or buyers that the value today has no relation to last year's value.

This program can also work very well with shopping centers. If the public can be persuaded that a new, upgraded shopping center exists where the old, unexciting center once stood, then the shoppers will come. And where there are shoppers there are tenants and higher rents. Again, the player *creates* value with an active development of his property,[33] a process which can greatly accelerate the realization of the rewards of real estate ownership.

A Whole New Use

As described later in this book, in 1980 our company bought a large industrial building for about $10/square foot. That was a fair price for what appeared to be a "white elephant."

Our plan was to attempt to alter both the image and usage of the building. Our idea was to change the building into a shopping center for factory outlet stores.

Our game plan involved very little renovation; all we really did was partition the factory building into separate areas for each store. The partitioning was plywood and chickenwire. The real effort was in leasing and promotion. We wanted to attract national manufacturers and, of course, lots of customers. Convincing the first few tenants entailed a lot of persuasion and some low-rent deals with "volume kickouts"—clauses in the leases stipulating that if the tenant didn't achieve a certain sales volume within an agreed period, it could cancel the lease. So, we had to deliver customers.

Through a determined campaign of advertising and promotion, we attempted to alter the public's image of the property. Our company screamed the news: "the *old* usage (industrial/low-end discounter) is gone, now there's a fantastic *new* shopping center."[34] Soon the word spread and the public discovered the transformation. With customers came more tenants and within a few years our rental rate/ square foot exceeded our purchase price/square foot. Needless to say, this project was a great financial success, in large part due to our ability to convince the world that our property was a *new* entity which just happened to be located where the *old* one had been.

Game Plan 4 is an attempt to boost value very quickly. It doesn't rely on or wait for traditional economic forces. It requires creativity and persistence. When it works, the financial return can be enormous.

Game Plan 5: Find the Cutting Edge

As in any other business, if you can be at the vanguard of new ideas and applications in the real estate game, you can sometimes hit a home run by acquiring a property at a price which reflects current—*not potential*—usage.

Condominium Conversions

The condominium/cooperative[35] conversion phenomenon is a case in point. When the first group of condominium converters came on the scene, apartment buildings were being valued according to their rent rolls. If a building had a net rent roll (before debt service) of $200,000/year, then its value was $200,000 divided by a capitalization rate (described in Chapter 3). If, for example, the "cap" rate was 11% then the apartment building was worth $200,000 divided by .11, or about $1,818,200.

Now along comes the converter. He values the building very differently: according to the number of apartment units (say 40) and the net retail price he can get by selling a unit (say, $60,000). Thus, in our example (based on actual deal), the condominium converter could buy for $1,818,200 and sell for $2,400,000—about a $600,000 profit. While the converter does have some conversion costs, these are relatively inexpensive, usually just the legal fees for preparation of the condominium documentation. And, the converter does bear the risk that he won't be able to sell the units; but in the early days of conversion this risk was nominal, for the building was bought at a price which was tied to its rent roll and so, worst case, the converter rented the units until they sold. The key was that the converter valued the property by an entirely different set of standards than the current owner and thus scored, in a sense, the minute he bought the building at the "rent-roll" price.

Eventually, however, apartment building owners wised up and began pricing their buildings as condo-conversions. The seller's rap became: "Forget the rent roll, I assure you these units will sell all day long at $60,000/per." So, no longer were apartment buildings valued at a lower set of standards than that used by condominium converters. In other words, condominium conversions are no longer on the cutting edge.

A similar example is the conversion of industrial-type buildings to factory outlet centers. When our company converted two industrial buildings to outlet centers in the early 1980s, the idea was still new and large industrial buildings were still priced according to industrial rentals, say $3 to $4/

square foot. But as the factory-outlet phenomenon spread, owners of well-located industrial buildings began to price them according to outlet-center rentals, say $6 to $7/square foot. No longer could we buy these buildings at prices calculated on rentals that were about half of what we could lease at. In other words, industrial-outlet center conversions are, in my opinion, no longer on the cutting edge.

Office and Retail Conversions

Some players are converting office and retail buildings to condominiums, that is, selling off individual offices or stores. Their game plan is:

1. to acquire buildings priced according to the rent roll and not the potential for condominium sale, assuming, of course, that the sale potential is higher, and/or

2. to profit on the spread between the wholesale price of the entire building and the retail price of the individual office or retail units they carve up.[36]

Today, office and retail buildings are still sold at prices which have nothing to do with their conversion potential. The reason is that the sale of individual office/retail units has not taken off[37] and most office buildings and shopping centers are still held and rented.

Perhaps office and/or retail condominiums will become increasingly popular and demand will drive up the price which people will pay for the condominium units. Then, the potential profit from conversion will increase to the point that some owners won't be able to resist converting. The result may be huge profits for those in a position to ride the first wave of conversions. But eventually the price of office and retail buildings will start to reflect their conversion potential and it will become difficult for the converter to score on a conversion project. The question, in other words, is whether office/retail conversions is now on the cutting edge? Should you attempt to acquire office and/or retail properties in anticipation of a conversion boom? Or should you direct your time, energy and resources into some other new idea? Needless to say, the cutting edge is not always easy to identify—it requires analysis, projection and the assumption of risk.

Dockominiums

We are seeing a new concept in Connecticut—dockominiums. For years, dock space (boat slips) was rented at some price per linear foot of the boat. As the demand for dock space increased, these rental prices also increased. So, demand for docks which could be owned also increased. And as demand increased, a local real estate player "condominiumized" a group of boat slips—and offered to sell individual slips. It is too early to tell whether this idea is a money-maker.

Time Sharing

About five years ago, time sharing, in which one buys ownership in a condominium for a specific period of time only, was very popular. For example, you could acquire a 1/12th interest in a condominium in Hawaii and be entitled to its use only for February of every year. Some real estate players made a lot of money by buying condominiums and then reselling them in several "time share" pieces.

Some people argue that time sharing is still a good business. Others say it has "topped out."

"Smart" Buildings

Some developers are today promoting the "intelligence" of their building, that is, the computerization of its various systems (for example, HVAC, elevator, security) as well as its adaptability to all sorts of communication tie-ins (phone, telex, etc.). These developers feel that these "smart" buildings will be more attractive to prospective tenants than "dumb" buildings and thus will achieve better rents and rent more quickly. In my opinion, this phenomenon is too new to determine (a) whether these buildings do, in fact, rent at higher rates and more quickly, and (b) if so, whether the rents and speed in renting justify the added costs of making a building "smart."

Self-Storage Facilities

Some players buy or lease buildings or warehouse space to convert to self-storage facilities. They acquire a large block of space,[38] partition it into individual storage areas and rent them[39] to individuals or businesses in need of additional storage space. Is this, in your opinion, an area on the cutting edge? Is it possible for you to find storage space at, say, $1 to $2/square foot that can be converted to individual units, which can then be rented at $5 or more/square foot? If so, you may want to explore this idea further, for the start-up costs (partitioning and advertising) are minimal and it is low-overhead business once it gets going.[40]

Specialized Shopping Centers

Some people believe that specialized "shopping centers"—where all the tenants are in the same type of business—are a thing of the future. Trammel Crow's Infomart in Dallas is an attempt to get all the computer manufacturers (and support companies) together into one building to display their wares to large-scale users, retailers and individual consumers.

In my opinion, there can be a tremendous profit in these specialized centers if the player can develop them in an existent, underutilized building, such as an unsuccessful shopping center or even an industrial or storage building. If the usage is unique and different enough (*a hook*) to attract the public in large numbers, then you've got a grand slam, for you'll lease in numbers far in excess of those used to value the property when you bought it.[41] The center itself becomes an event—half shopping center, half public attraction. The smart developer will attempt to play on this fact with displays, games, food, etc. All that's necessary is to figure out what type of specialized shopping center can be created and what will capture the public's interest.

Anything Else You Think Makes Sense

The great thing about the cutting edge is that it is constantly moving—which means tremendous opportunity for the creative real estate player. I have attempted to illustrate some ideas which are now or have been (or perhaps will be) on the cutting edge of the real estate game. But these are just some food for thought. There are hundreds of new ideas floating around, ready to be implemented and capitalized on. Think about the needs, desires and trends of the future. How can these needs, desires and trends be integrated into your real estate game plan?

Game Plan 6: Anything That Works

There are no right or wrong ideas in the real estate game. Success in the real estate game is not subjective—it's very objective: how do your deals work financially? Whatever works for you is by definition "right."
And things constantly change—what worked yesterday may not work tomorrow. And change means opportunity!

Notes to Chapter 1

1.   Meaning here any income-producing property other than residential.

2.   You may wish to read Dave Glubetich's *The Monopoly Game* (available directly from Glubetich at 12 Gregory Lane, Pleasant Hill, California).

3.   If you are interested in multi-family housing, you may enjoy reading William Nickerson's *How I Turned $1,000 into Three million in Real Estate in My Spare Time*, (New York: Simon & Schuster, 1969) and its update *How I Turned $1,000 into Five Million in My Spare Time* (New York: Simon & Schuster, 1980).

4.   For example, if a player has $20,000 available to him and he can buy four single-family houses with 95% financing, then he can acquire four $100,000 houses. Even if the inflation rate is 4% (as it was in 1984), this player's return on investment in the first year will be 80%: Inflation increases the value of each house by 4% or $4,000 x 4 = $16,000. $16,000 divided by $20,000 = 80%. (If the inflation rate were 10%, the player's return would be $40,000 divided by $20,000 or 200%!)

5.   Location must be considered.

6.   Some players buy and rent luxury homes or apartments. As the number of potential renters and buyers of these properties is limited, the player's risk is greater.

7.   As with anything else, a poor economy can affect demand; in bad times people double up or move in with family, depressing demand.

8.   Remember, refinancing is another way to get to your equity.

9.   Once again, the state of the economy can be a factor and in times of high interest rates, demand to buy will be down. *But*, to some extent, those people who can't buy must rent, so the player who can't sell (or won't sell at reduced prices) because of a poor economy may be in a strong position to rent.

10. Compare the following discussions about players who attempt to *create value* and thus have no external ceiling on their returns.

11. In Chapter 3 we will discuss the relationship between the cash flow (or loss) from a property and the amount of financing—what I call the "trade-off."

12. Even though they may be earning more than 100% per year on their money!

13. I am not using "undervalued" to mean only underpriced. More common are properties which cannot command their

true value for one or more of the following reasons: the house may be jammed with old dark furniture; the color of the house may be awful; basic maintenance may have been deferred, etc. The point is that these houses are actually worth more than they sell for. It's just that they don't get their price because they distort the market system of pricing (demand-supply) by artificially depressing demand, i.e., they depress people's interest in the house. These were exactly the type of houses that I was looking for, however, because I knew that I could buy and resell at a profit, quickly bringing to the surface the house's true value without spending a lot of money.

14. I avoided properties with major structural problems.

15. After a thorough building inspection and an estimate of my renovation costs.

16. Painting, installing skylights, new windows—changes dealing with the *look* of the house. Structural changes are costly, risky and time consuming.

17. A net worth of maybe $100,000, which was about $99,000 more than mine.

18. If I knew anyone to ask to cosign, I would have offered him one-third of the deal just for his signature. As it was, my partner took half (which I was glad to give up since without him I could not have bought the house).

19. I was able to convince the construction lender to bill us quarterly, which meant we had 90 days before the first interest payment was due. Had the bank decided to bill us monthly we would have had to make an interest payment in 30 days, which could have brought down our little "house of cards."

20. The lender was quite comfortable with the appraisals of three reputable brokers; he did not require anything from a certified appraiser.

21. We had kept our word to the cosigner, for his obligation to the bank expired when we repaid the $60,000 construction loan.

22. For the tax treatment of overfinance proceeds, see Chapter 5.

23. I have oversimplified the development process by not mentioning risk.

24. After having done some preliminary homework to assure yourself that the sale price is reasonable in light of the probable use(s) of the land.

25. Some developers are very successful at "pre-leasing" buildings, that is, signing up the tenant before the building is even built.

26. Plus, there is a lot of risk: construction problems, time delays, sluggish rental demand.

27. You would, of course, first show the land to Burger King and get their approval of the site.

28. Your profit is the spread between your land rental and your debt service, insurance and taxes.

29. A relationship with a national tenant can be used in a variety of ways—not just new construction. For example, if you know that a certain company will lease X square feet of existing space at $Y/square foot, you can go into the marketplace and attempt to acquire an appropriate building at a price at which you will be able to turn a profit given the tenant you will immediately put into the building.

30. Usually a large, well-known user who will attract both people and tenants to the center.

31. This game plan is not a dollar-for-dollar-type approach; the goal is to increase the value many times the amount invested to effect the illusion.

32. Some real estate players are very adept at using press releases, events and other public relations techniques to convince the world that a new property has risen over the ashes of the old.

33. The normal forces of appreciation are just too slow for these players.

34. In this case, we didn't want to *totally* change the public's perception, for part of our campaign was that the building—formerly a *factory*—now housed factory outlets and shopping there was tantamount to buying off the *factory* floor.

35. In a cooperative, the owner of the property is a corporation. Each tenant/owner owns stock in the corporation and holds a proprietary lease to his "co-op." In a condominium, each person actually owns his unit (in connected units, generally from the inside walls in) and some percentage of the common areas—driveways, land, recreational facilities, etc.

36. This spread may exist even when a property is priced in light of its conversion potential—as are most apartment buildings today—and is the reason there are still residential condominium conversions taking place.

37. There does seem, however, to be a growing number of medical office condominiums.

38. At wholesale prices.

39. At retail rates.

40. I know one group of players making about $200,000/year on a self-storage facility which they created in about 45,000 square feet of space rented from our company.

41. This is an example of the combined use of Game Plans 4 and 5.

2
Real Estate: A Wealth Generator

Market Forces

There are powerful forces driving up the value of real estate which will contribute to your efforts, almost no matter what you do. These forces are behind the upward climb in values which has been the history of real estate in the United States. (There have been dips along the way, but keeping an overview, these "downtimes" have been relatively short term.)

Supply and Demand

Basic economics teaches us that price is a function of the amount of something that exists (supply) and the desire for it (demand).

We all know that they're not making any more land. In addition, the hurdles (e.g., cost; zoning and other governmental regulations; public opposition) to constructing more buildings on what land is available have increased. At the same time, population continues to increase in leaps and bounds. The result is more people chasing an increasingly scarce commodity or, in supply-demand terms, demand outstripping supply, resulting in price increases.

We can expect the forces of supply and demand to continue to drive up the value of real estate as there is absolutely nothing on the horizon to indicate a change in the factors motoring the supply-demand upward push.

Inflation

There are many reasons for inflation, most of which, in my opinion, have become ingrained within our economy and are here to stay. Therefore, in my view, although the annual rate of inflation may vary from year to year, the fact of continuing price increases, in other words inflation, is with us for the foreseeable future.

During periods of high inflation it makes sense to have a good portion of your money invested in a tangible asset which at the least keeps pace with the rate of inflation, for during these periods, one must ask whether interest received on money in the bank even keeps pace with inflation. If not, then the buying power of money in the bank decreases. In addition, one should analyze the *after-tax* return on money in the bank. For example, if you are in a 25% tax bracket and keep your money in a money market account earning 10%, the after-tax return on your money is actually 7.5%.[1] Based on the rate of inflation, your money in the bank may actually be losing buying power. When the inflation rate exceeds the after-tax return on money in the bank, it makes sense to move your cash into tangible assets such as real estate. (There are, of course, noneconomic reasons—e.g., the speed with which one can produce "cash" in the event of a need or an opportunity—for keeping some portion of your wealth in liquid assets. The point is to be aware of the eroding force of inflation and to make an informed, reasoned decision as to what percentage of your assets you wish to be liquid.)

Inflation forces the value of real estate up year after year almost no matter what you do, because prices of tangible assets generally increase during periods of inflation. It is just the kind of phenomenon you want working for you. It can be an extremely powerful wealth generator, especially when viewed in conjunction with the "financeability" of real estate ("leverage") discussed below.

The Psychology of Expectations

I believe that there is a force pushing up real estate prices, which is related to but also independent of the phenomena of supply-demand and inflation.

Real estate, in my opinion, is the "golden boy" of the investment world, that is, most people view real estate investment as the best and quickest way to get rich. There are *many* reasons for this public appeal:

1. the many stories and books about self-made real estate millionaires

2. the visibility of the rich and their real estate—the newest national real estate idol, Donald Trump, has generated considerable publicity for his Trump Towers development on New York City's Fifth Avenue and the development has in turn generated a lot of publicity for him

3. the individual personal observations and experiences of the general public—watching real estate price increases in communities across the country

4. the common (and, in my opinion, accurate) perception that real estate is understandable and manageable. (Contrast, for example, the general perception most people have of the commodities/futures markets or the municipal bond market.) The simple fact that it is visible also helps its image.

The by-product of this favorable attitude toward real estate is that there is a force pushing up real estate prices, independent of economic factors. This force is what I call "psychology of expectations"—that is, I believe people will buy real estate at ever increasing prices because they perceive that others will someday do the same, earning them a profit on their investment. Because so many people expect real estate prices to continue to rise, they will buy "on the futures," driving up prices *today* in the belief that others will buy at increased prices *tomorrow*.

While this phenomenon is hard to quantify, it is nevertheless important to recognize as another major force, working along with you (once you've acquired real estate) to increase real estate prices—again, almost no matter what you do.[2]

A Money Machine

As discussed in the Introduction, there are many different ways to invest your time and energy. One advantage to investing it in the real estate game is that you are working to acquire assets which have "lives" of their own.

If you earn a salary, your hard work goes into your job, and if you do a good job you get the right to earn that salary again next year. If, on the other hand, you are able to direct that time and energy into building something—an asset which will survive your effort—then you may have something working for you. And, if that asset has a "life" of its own such that it produces money—year after year—*with no additional effort on your part*, then you've really got something great working for you. For, now your hard work has earned you something more than just the right to work hard again next year; it's earned you a "money machine."

A successful real estate project is a money machine. Once working, it generates cash flow (and appreciates in value) with little or no effort on your part. It works when you are on vacation, when you're pursuing new properties. It gives you freedom in that your time and energy no longer have to be tied to making a living. If you choose, you can pursue other interests or attempt to create additional money machines and build an empire.

The Financeability of Real Estate: Leverage

The greatest thing going for the real estate player is the financeability of real estate, the ability to acquire real estate with a large percentage of borrowed money, what is commonly termed "leverage." Like a lever, which permits its user to move items many times heavier than what he normally could, leverage creates the opportunity for the real estate owner to earn a return on his or her equity many times greater than that equity would earn in other investments.

For a variety of reasons,[3] lenders of all types feel comfortable lending money against real estate. (In some states the loan is secured by a mortgage; in other states a deed of trust is used.) This fact is a fantastic opportunity for the real estate player, for it opens the door to purchases with little, if any, of the investor's own money. For this reason, understanding the principles of financing is the first step to success in the real estate game.

Notes to Chapter 2

1.   As someone in the 25% bracket pays taxes of 25 cents for every $1.00 of gross income, someone earning a 10% return pays 2.5% in taxes and actually nets (after taxes) only 7.5%.

2.   I have seen many sophisticated real estate sellers and brokers play on a prospective buyer's or tenant's "psychology of expectations." For example, an undecided buyer or tenant may often be persuaded to act with a casual: "Frankly, I'm just as happy to sit with it; it will probably be worth that much more next spring."

3.   Some of the reasons are: real estate stays put and thus the lender will always know where to find it in the event of a problem (compare diamonds or gold); real estate is relatively easy to value or appraise (compare collectibles, such as rare coins); commercial real estate has a built-in fallback for debt

reduction, the rent roll; the laws of foreclosure against real estate are well established (laws covering the lender's rights to recapture certain personal property are sometimes unclear).

3

Financing:
Anything Is Possible

Understanding Leverage

By leveraging an acquisition of real estate, that is, by buying with a great percentage of borrowed money, an investor is
able to obtain an asset valued at five to 10 times (or more) the
investor's cash. Presuming the value of the asset rises, the
return to the investor's cash will thus be five to 10 times the
percentage increase in the value of the asset.

For example, if you buy a house for $100,000 with $20,000 of
your own money and $80,000 of borrowed funds, you control
an asset five times the value of your actual cash investment.
Now, if the value of the house increases 5% per year, next
year your house is worth $105,000 *but* your return on cash is
five times as great, or 25% per year ($5,000 increase/$20,000
cash invested = 25% return).

Analyzing the Trade-Off

You could easily improve on the return on cash in the above
example: if you can convince a lender to loan you $90,000

against your $100,000 house instead of $80,000, then the return on your cash investment after one year is 50% ($5,000 increase/$10,000 cash invested = 50% return). You can now begin to see how game players can earn more than 100% per year on their cash (if any) invested in a property.

But, as with anything, there is a trade-off: the more you leverage a deal—the greater the percentage of financing—the higher your debt payments. Not that higher debt payments are necessarily bad—even if the higher debt payment results in a negative cash flow (when your gross rentals from a property are less than operating costs plus debt service), you still may want the additional financing.

In order to analyze the trade-off, you must not only consider the increased debt service on your prospective deal but also the value of the cash you won't need to use if you choose the larger loan. If the extra cash allows you to do an additional deal, you may well wish to live with a negative cash flow.

As an example, suppose Smith has $30,000 to invest in real estate and he locates a small commercial building which can be bought for $100,000. Smith's lender is willing to finance up to 90% of the purchase at a loan which floats two points over the prime rate (9.5% as of this writing), with a "straight amortization"[1] over 10 years. The first year's debt payments on a $90,000 loan will be approximately $10,350 interest[2] ($90,000 x 11.5%) plus $9,000 principal ($90,000 divided by 10) or $19,350. Assuming that the net rental[3] from this building is $17,500, Smith has a first-year negative cash flow[4] of $1,850 if he takes the 90% loan. If, on the other hand, Smith uses all of his $30,000 cash and thus only needs a $70,000 loan, the first-year debt service will be $15,050 ($70,000 x 11.5% = $8,050 + $7,000 [$70,000 divided by 10] = $15,050) and the property will generate a positive cash flow of $2,450. Should Smith take the 90% loan?

Smith should consider the following in making his decision:

1. part of his negative cash flow is loan repayment. In the first example, without the $9,000 payment, Smith would have a $7,150 positive cash flow. He may thus factor out the loan repayment, considering it instead a form of

compulsory saving in that some day (on sale or refinance) he will get it back (assuming that the value of the property at least stays constant). On the other hand, perhaps Smith does not choose to save his money in this manner.

2.   his annual debt service (and thus negative cash flow), which will decrease as he works down the outstanding principal balance of the $90,000 loan

3.   how much his rents can be increased when leases expire

4.   his projections as to what he thinks interest rates will do in the future. Can he carry the property if he takes the 90% loan and prime increases two to three points?

5.   the after-tax cost of the negative cash flow, as the negative cash flow may be[5] a deduction for tax purposes (a loss)

6.   what he can do with the additional $20,000 cash he'll have if he takes the 90% loan. Can he buy one or two more similar properties? If so, what is the value of owning each in terms of potential cash flow, appreciation and tax shelter?

The answers to Smith's questions will vary greatly depending upon the specifics of a deal and the availability of other deals. Having made that statement, I believe that the great majority of successful game players would take the 90% loan, worry about the negative cash flow when they have to make the debt payments (monthly or perhaps quarterly) and try to buy two similar $100,000 properties with 90% financing.

Understanding the Concepts

Interest

The rate you pay for the money you borrow is, of course, termed interest. Up until about five years ago, one could obtain a long-term fixed-interest loan. Today these loans are much more difficult to obtain,[6] for lenders are very concerned about predicting interest rates and thus being locked into fixed rates over the long term. Therefore, you now have to analyze your deal in terms of financing with an interest rate that will fluctuate or change after 5-7 years (pretty much the longest time that lenders will fix rates).

Most commercial loans—also called "variable rate loans"—offered today have a floating, or adjustable, interest rate. The interest rate is usually pegged to the prime rate (or some other standard) and it moves either immediately as the prime moves or within some short-term time frame thereafter (such as monthly or annually). Fixed-rate loans are available, but most of these freeze the interest rate for only five years. Therefore, the loans available, while perhaps having a duration of 20 or more years, will have some built-in procedure allowing the lender to change the interest rate after a stipulated period (and usually, every X years thereafter).

There is a great variety of interest rate packages being offered and the real estate player should develop a feel for his options. Under the heading of interest rates, one must consider:

1. the initial loan rate (fixed rate loans will always start with a higher rate than variable rate loans because the lender is plugging in an uncertainty factor)

2. how long the loan rate is frozen

3. how frequently the loan rate can be changed and by what procedure

4. the standard (e.g., prime rate, treasury bill rate) that the loan rate is tied to

5. whether there is a "cap," or maximum, at which the interest rate can be changed—both periodically and over the term of the loan

6. whether there is a prepayment penalty—a dollar amount that a borrower must pay if he elects to repay the loan before some defined date, and

7. the origination fee (charge by the bank for granting you the loan) or "points,"[7] for the loan, if any.

Amortization

Amortization is the term used to describe the reduction of the principal amount borrowed. Some loans have no amortization; they are called appropriately "interest-only" loans. Other loans are interest-only for some period of time and then amortization kicks in.

It is important to understand the rate of amortization of the loans available to you. "Straight amortization" is generally the repayment of the debt in equal annual amounts over the term of the loan. (Thus, the "straight amortization" of a $90,000 10-year loan means that the borrower repays the debt $9,000/year.) Sometimes the debt is amortized over a longer period than the term of the loan. For example, the lender may suggest (or you may request) a 10-year loan with the debt being amortized over 25 years. With this loan you will repay 1/25 of the principal annually, with 15/25 of the debt payable in a lump sum, or "balloon," payment when the term of the loan is up after year 10. The advantage of this type of loan to the borrower is that the annual principal payments are much less than if the debt were amortized in full over the term of the loan; the disadvantage is that the borrower pays more total interest because the debt (against which the interest is calculated) is not being reduced as quickly as with a straight amortization loan.

"Self-liquidating" loans describe fixed-payment loans (with fixed-interest rates) which work the debt down to zero as of the expiration date of the loan. Most residential loans were self-liquidating until a few years ago when lenders became nervous about fixed-interest rates. This type of loan is generally not available for a commercial project unless the amortization is very short and then it is probably undesirable to a prospective borrower.

The term "constant" is used to describe the percentage of annual loan payments—principal and interest—to the original principal balance of the loan. A 15% "constant," for example, means that the combination of interest and principal which the borrower pays annually on, say, a $1,000,000 loan is $150,000.

Loan Priority and Subordination

Real estate loans are secured by mortgages or deeds of trust. In either case, a document is recorded which informs the world of the lender's interest in the real estate standing as security. (From this point forward, I will refer only to mortgages, although the same principles apply to deeds of trust.)

When there is more than one mortgage against a piece of real estate, it is critical to identify the priority of the mortgages, for in the event the borrower defaults, the lender with the higher priority mortgage gets his money out first. Depending on the sales price realized—foreclosure sales generally result in depressed prices—a subordinate lender may lose some or all of his loan;[8] therefore, identifying the order of repayment in the event of foreclosure is very important.

Generally, the sooner, chronologically, a mortgage is recorded, the higher its priority. Thus, the first (in time) mortgage recorded is the first (in priority) mortgage and so on. That is why a mortgage lender should always search the land records before loaning against a piece of real estate in order to discover any previously recorded mortgages (or, for that matter, liens of any sort, such as judgments) which by reason of their prior recording would have a priority over the lender's mortgage.

The concern with priority does not, of course, mean that lenders are necessarily deterred from taking a second, third or fourth etc., position against real estate. Second mortgages, for example, are very common. The lender of a subordinate mortgage will, however, want to assure himself that the real estate has a value sufficient to cover both the prospective loan amount and the outstanding balance on the higher priority mortgage(s) in the event of a foreclosure sale. The secondary lender also will almost always charge an interest rate higher than that available for first mortgages to compensate for the greater risk.

There is a fairly common exception to the rule that the earlier a mortgage is recorded the higher its priority. In certain instances, a lender will agree to *subordinate* his mortgage to another mortgage, which means that he voluntarily pushes the priority of his mortgage back behind a new (later-recorded) mortgage. This is accomplished by execution of a subordination agreement which refers to the new mortgage and specifically subordinates, or lowers, the priority of the old mortgage to of that of the new mortgage.

Subordination is probably most common with respect to land purchases. Say, for example, that Seller wants to sell his land to Buyer, and Seller is willing to take some portion of the purchase price back as a purchase-money mortgage.[9] Buyer purchases Seller's land for $300,000 with $100,000 cash and a $200,000 note to Seller, which Seller secures with a mortgage against the land. As this mortgage will generally be recorded immediately after the deed (see Chapter 7) from Seller to Buyer is recorded, it will have priority over any other mortgage which Buyer subsequently attempts to place against the land. But Buyer knows that having Seller's mortgage as a "first"[10] is a problem, for Buyer wants to develop the land and very few construction lenders will take any position other than a first. (The same applies to "takeout" lenders, a general catch-all term that refers to permanent lenders whose loan replaces or "takes out" the short-term construction loan.) Therefore, in his negotiations with Seller prior to purchase, Buyer must take the position that Seller's mortgage will have to be subordinated to a loan or loans to be subsequently placed against the property. Buyer may have to explain to Seller that without this agreement Seller's offer of purchase-money financing is of no value to Buyer, for as soon as Buyer attempts to develop the land and obtain a construction loan, he will have to pay off Seller's loan in order to obtain a release of Seller's mortgage and allow the construction lender to obtain a first mortgage against the land. If Seller agrees, the mortgage deed from Buyer to Seller will contain a provision providing either for its automatic (without further documentation) subordination (to, for example, a "construction mortgage") or, an agreement by Seller to execute at a subsequent time a subordination agreement which is recorded and which subordinates Seller's mortgage to the specific mortgage(s) that Buyer later places against the property.

Knowledge of the principles of subordination, mixed with some creativity and salesmanship, can help you to "cash out" of deals (buy real estate with none of your own money) and, in some cases, to "overfinance" (borrow more than the total cost of a deal). Let me give you an example (an actual deal):

Seller has a building for sale which Buyer would like to buy. The asking price is $425,000, and the building needs a total renovation. Seller is willing to take back a mortgage of $375,000 and Buyer convinces Seller that while the offered financing is certainly very attractive, it only has value if Seller is willing to subordinate this mortgage to construction and then permanent (take-out) financing. Otherwise, Buyer will have no ability to obtain construction money to perform the needed extensive renovations. Seller is unsure but is eventually convinced by Buyer's argument that Seller's position is not affected by the subordination for the construction money (which will be used for renovations) will increase the value of the real estate by at least the amount of the renovation dollars and thus there will be no change (or perhaps an increase) in the amount of real estate value securing Seller's mortgage.

Buyer purchases Seller's building with $50,000 cash (which he borrowed short term from a local commercial lender) with Seller taking back a $375,000 mortgage. The mortgage deed includes a clause stating that "Seller will execute whatever subordination documents are necessary to subordinate Seller's mortgage to a construction (and then a permanent) mortgage to be placed against the real estate."

Before going to contract, Buyer had engaged an architect and general contractor to give him an estimate on renovation costs, and he learned that he could get the renovation done for $350,000. Nevertheless, he convinces a lender to give him a $450,000 construction loan based not solely on the cost of construction but also on the value of the completed project (appraisals are discussed later on). Given the costs of this project ($425,000 plus $350,000) Buyer has little trouble convincing the lender that the completed project will be worth $800,000 or more and that therefore a construction-type loan of $450,000 is very secure so long as the lender has a first position. (Remember, this means that the construction lender actually has $800,000 securing $450,000, for his money comes out first in the event of a foreclosure.) The lender agrees and Seller executes the appropriate subordination document,[11] giving the construction (and eventually the take-out) lender the first position.

Now let's see what Buyer has done. He has obtained $450,000 from the construction lender, of which he needs only $350,000 to complete the renovation. With the additional $100,000 he receives, he repays the short-term $50,000 loan which he took to buy the real estate and puts 50,000 tax-free dollars in his pocket.[13] The upshot is that Buyer bought and renovated this project with none of his own money and put 50,000 after-tax dollars in his pocket. While Buyer must now meet higher mortgage payments (basically the payments on the extra $100,000), he has $50,000 to the good which can be used to earn interest or to make money in another deal.

I know of numerous variations on the above example—in each case the buyer bought real estate with none of his own money and often overfinanced, putting tax-free cash into his own pocket. The key is understanding how to use subordination to your advantage.

Assumability and "Wraps"

Sometimes a buyer can take over the existent financing on a piece of real estate. On occasion, for example, you may hear a seller asking for "$200,000 to the mortgage." This asking price implies that the seller has an *assumable* mortgage (or mortgages), which is transferable to the buyer, and that the seller is seeking $200,000 cash above the assumable financing. If the assumable mortgage(s) has an outstanding balance of $800,000 and the buyer pays $200,000 "cash to the mortgage," then the selling price is $1,000,000.

The advantages to the buyer of real estate with an assumable mortgage are that:

1. Usually the assumable mortgage(s) will have a below-market interest rate. The mortgage may be several years old[13] and thus may have a rate several points below the current market rate. The flip side, however, is that the seller may well be trying to capitalize on the below-market financing with an inflated sale price.

2. An existent mortgage(s) saves the buyer the need to obtain a mortgage at the desired amount (and eliminates the risk that he will not be able to get such a mortgage), as well as acquisition and closing costs (of the loan), such as origination fees, legal fees, appraisal, mortgage, brokerage.

3. At some time after buying, the buyer may put the real estate on the market and thus become the seller. If the mortgage(s) in question was assumable once, it is probably assumable again. (Because this is not necessarily true, the note and mortgage documents must be reviewed.) Therefore, the original buyer—now a seller—has attractive financing to offer along with his real estate. The result is that the real estate may well be much more marketable than similar real estate without this financing.

Let me give you an example of an actual deal which occurred about four years ago and which illustrates the principles of assumability and subordination.

Buyer purchased an apartment building from Seller for $900,000. Seller took back a purchase-money mortgage of $700,000, which he agreed would go behind a first mortgage of not more than $100,000 to be put on at closing. So, Buyer bought this building with $100,000 cash,[14] a $100,000 first mortgage and the $700,000 purchase-money second mortgage. As part of the sales negotiations, however, Buyer did something very smart: instead of arguing with Seller over the asking price (Seller was asking $900,000), Buyer agreed to the price but in return obtained the following concessions in the purchase-money mortgage:

1. that it be behind a certain amount at closing (Buyer asked for $200,000; Seller would only agree to $100,000)

2. that it be subordinated in the future to additional construction/take-out financing so long as the new money borrowed would "go into improving the property'

3. that the amount of the mortgage(s) which Seller would subordinate to could be increased by $25,000/year to take account for the increased value in the real estate by reason of appreciation

4. that the purchase-money loan would be fixed at 9% and that the loan would be self-liquidating over 30 years

5. that the mortgage would be forever assumable (with no requirements as to the financial standing of Buyer's buyer) and that as soon as Buyer sold, Seller would execute a release of Buyer from the underlying loan obligation of $700,000 (or whatever the outstanding principal balance was at the time).

With this very attractive financing package, Buyer developed his game plan: hold the property for two or three years and during that time make a concerted effort to increase the rents and improve the rent roll. Then, with the income of the property up, put it on the market along with the attractive financing and attempt to "score" on the sale. Buyer did just that. Two years after purchasing the apartment building Buyer put it on the market, offering prospective buyers 95% financing, at below-market rates. Soon thereafter Buyer (from now on Buyer 1) sold the property to Buyer 2 for $1,400,000 payable as follows:

1. $25,000 cash

2. $175,000 first mortgage[15]

3. $700,000 second mortgage (Seller's) and a

4. $500,000 third mortgage from Buyer 2 to Buyer 1 at a rate of 11%, self-liquidating over 10 years.

For his efforts Buyer 1 was now entitled to receive $6,887 per month for the next 10 years by simply opening his mailbox and depositing Buyer 2's payments on the $500,000 third mortgage.[16] As it happened, however, Buyer 1 had made an error in judgment as to Buyer 2. Given the percentage of financing to the sales price, Buyer 1 had to consider Buyer 2's ability to carry the property and make all the mortgage payments even with a negative cash flow. Buyer 2 began missing payments on the third mortgage. Accordingly Buyer 1 had to threaten to foreclose. Eventually Buyer 2 got a partner and together they bought out Buyer 1's mortgage, Buyer 1 thereby receiving about $150,000 cash in the year following his sale to Buyer 2. All in all, Buyer 1 still made a very nice deal, which for the most part was made possible by his obtaining and using attractive financing from Seller.

Some creative game players have attempted to turn below-market financing into assumable financing even though such was not the intention of the lender. Mortgages which a lender does not wish to be assumable should include "due on sale" language.[17] The language varies from state-to-state, but it is usually something like: "This mortgage may not be assumed and is due on the sale of the mortgaged property." Without this language, I believe that a mortgagor (the lender is the mortgagee and the borrower is the mortgagor) has a very good argument that he has an assumable mortgage. But even with the due-on-sale language some game players have attempted to *create* "assumable financing." (When there is a great interest rate differential between the loan rate and the existent market rate, assumable financing adds value to a property.)

These game players have all taken basically the same tack: they have all attempted to structure the transfer of their property so that it is arguably not a "sale" as covered by the due-on-sale clause within their mortgage. They have attempted to achieve this end through various mechanisms; one is an installment sales contract whereby the buyer and the seller enter a long-term contract, which is recorded instead of a deed. The contract provides for payments from the buyer to the seller over a period of time which may range from a couple of years to 30 years. At the end of this period, and assuming that the buyer has made all contract payments, the seller then transfers a deed to the buyer. (Often this deed is executed by the seller in advance and held in escrow, to be released by the escrow agent upon the buyer establishing that he has made the requisite payments.) If the lender of the seller's existent mortgage attempts to call the loan based on due-on-sale language in the mortgage, the seller argues that there has been no sale as there has been no passage of title. The seller argues that all that has happened is that a contract has been entered for a closing of title X years in the future.

But what has really happened? I believe that the lender can make a strong argument that the seller has really "sold" and simply financed the "purchase." In other words, notwithstanding that the deed is held in escrow somewhere, ownership has really changed hands and the buyer's contract payments are in reality debt payments on purchase-money "financing."

Such questions have led to litigation, and the courts of different states have decided differently. As a buyer[18] or a seller[19] about to enter this type of deal, you should check with a knowledgeable real estate attorney about decisions within your state and the best way to structure a deal of this type.

In the previous example, the purpose of the installment contract was to create assumable financing, which adds to the marketability and value of the seller's property. But the experienced seller may also attain an extra benefit by way of an interest rate spread between the existent financing and the financing he extends to the buyer. An example may help to illustrate this point.

Seller owns an office building. When he bought the building 10 years ago, he obtained a $400,000 first mortgage at an interest rate of 7% and with straight amortization over a term of 20 years. Therefore, there is now an outstanding balance of

$200,000. The mortgage contains a due-on-sale clause. Seller wants to sell the building to Buyer for $700,000 and Buyer is willing to purchase at this price if Seller can provide an attractive financing package.

Seller proposes the following: $100,000 cash and the balance to be financed by Seller at a fixed rate of 13% plus straight amortization over 10 years. (Note that Seller has structured the amortization from Buyer such that Seller is paid off at the same rate as he must pay off his lender.) But since Seller's mortgage has a due-on-sale clause and Seller can only make this offer by keeping that mortgage in place, Seller suggests an installment contract. The contract will be for 10 years and will provide for payments as follows: $100,000 on contract signing and the balance ($600,000) payable monthly in the exact same manner as if Buyer were a borrower of $600,000 repaying it over 10 years (straight amortization) with 13% interest on the unpaid balance. The only negative for Buyer is that he doesn't have legal title until the end of the 10 years, although his contract with Seller may be recorded and thereby negate some of the risks of not having title. The advantages for Buyer are related to the financing: he's obtained almost 90% financing at a competitive interest rate and without the costs of an appraisal, points or loan closing.

Seller, too, is satisfied. He has sold his property for what is presumably a good price *and* he is making money on the spread on interest between his existent mortgage (7%) and the rate Buyer is paying (13%). On $200,000 (the outstanding balance of the first mortgage), this interest rate spread earns him $12,000/year (6% spread x $200,000) for doing nothing more than creating an assumable mortgage—remember, Seller hasn't even loaned this money (*he's earning* 13% on the $400,000 he takes back); he is effectively earning money on the lender's money. The only one really unhappy is the lender.

Seller has created a "wrap" of 13% interest around the $200,000, 7% interest first-mortgage loan. This wrap terminology is used whenever a seller extends financing to a buyer at a rate in excess of existent financing which the seller keeps in place. Another example would be a sale from Seller to Buyer with Seller taking back a $1 million mortgage and keeping in place a $500,000 first mortgage to his lender.[20] Assume that Seller is repaying $500,000 at 10% and he loans the $1,000,000 to Buyer at 12%.[21] Seller has "wrapped" the existent first mortgage and thus the mortgage from Buyer to Seller is termed a "wrap-around," and it is technically a second mortgage because the existent mortgage from Seller to the lender has the first position. Again, Seller may put this package together to make his property both more marketable and valuable as well as to earn money on the spread on the interest rate.

Recourse V. Nonrecourse

Earlier I mentioned deficiency judgments, which are basically legal judgments obtained by a lender against a borrower for the difference between the amount of an outstanding loan and the net sale price of a foreclosed property. As an example, if Jones borrowed $200,000 from Smith and secured the loan with his house (that is, Jones executes a $200,000 mortgage against his house) and Jones defaults, Smith will sue Jones in foreclosure. Smith must attempt to sell the house according to the specific procedures[22] established by the state in which the house is located. Suppose Smith follows the required procedures but can only sell the house for $100,000; in addition Smith has costs of foreclosure of $10,000. Smith now has a deficiency judgment against Jones for $110,000, which he can attempt to collect against Jones' other assets. This scenario presumes that the loan is recourse (and that the property is in a state which permits deficiency actions), which essentially means that the lender has a recourse—a deficiency action—against a borrower when the amount realized on a foreclosed property doesn't cover the outstanding balance of the lender's loan plus costs of foreclosure. A nonrecourse loan, on the other hand, is secured only by the real estate; there is no possibility of the lender suing the borrower in a deficiency action. A nonrecourse loan is identified as such by language in the loan documents to the effect of: "This loan is intended to be nonrecourse as against the borrower and in the event of default hereunder, the lender's only security for the herein loan shall be the mortgaged property."

How do you get a nonrecourse loan?

1. Always ask for it.

2. Consider the different lenders available to you; in any area of the country nonrecourse loans are more likely to be available from nonbank lenders (with the possible exception of the large, sophisticated banking institutions) such as insurance companies, pension funds and credit companies. The problem is that most of these lenders are not very interested in loans under $5,000,000.

3. Offer the lender an attractive enough package such that he will be willing to take the increased risk of looking only to the property for the collection of the debt; in other words, waive recourse requirements. Examples of what you might offer the lender are a better-than-usual interest rate; a higher-than-usual debt coverage ratio;[23] a piece of the action (joint venture or equity participation).

4. Become a very good customer of a lender; do everything you can to nurture and strengthen the relationship.

Even if a nonrecourse loan is available to you, you should analyze whether the loan as a whole is better than a recourse loan if the other terms of the recourse loan are preferable. For example, is a $1 million recourse loan with a 25-year term and a 12% interest rate which is fixed for five years and then floats 1 1/2% over prime more or less desirable than a $900,000 nonrecourse loan with a 20-year term and an interest rate that floats 2 1/2% over prime? The answer will, of course, depend upon the specific deal; the only point here is to analyze all parts of the loan package and not simply the risk factor, i.e., recourse v. nonrecourse.[24]

Appraisals and Construction Budgets

The use of appraisals and construction budgets in obtaining financing is often overlooked by the beginning real estate player.

Appraisals

Quite frequently a prospective lender will request an appraisal of the property to be purchased. Especially when the loan-to-purchase price ratio is high, the lender will probably want an appraisal of the property. Sometimes the purpose is to define the true value of an existent property—in order to insure that the purchase price reflects market value. Other times the purpose is to identify the future value of a project to be developed, such as a new building or a renovation. In all cases the appraised value will be an important factor in determining the amount of financing available to you.

Appraisals are "expert" opinions of the market value of an existent or future property. As with any opinion, the value can vary greatly depending upon the appraiser's approach and assumptions. It thus makes sense for the real estate player to learn the basics of appraisal procedure.

Most commercial appraisals use an "income" approach, a method which attempts to evaluate the present value of the right to receive $X over Y years, adding in some amount for the residual value of the property at the end of Y years. The income approach attempts to identify current and future net income (before debt service) and to put a present value on this income stream (and expected residual worth of the property). Many appraisers will perform this valuation by use of a "cap," or capitalization, rate. A capitalization rate is a percentage which, when divided into a property's current net income, gives one a rough idea of the present value of the property's projected income stream (and residual value). The cap rate will vary from time to time as interest rates (and other factors) change, but at any point in time the cap rate used by most appraisers in a geographic area will not vary by more than a point or so. As an example, the cap rate used today by most appraisers in my area is between 10% and 11%, so that if we find a property with a $100,000 net income (income before debt service), we can roughly calculate that an appraiser will come in at a value between $909,090 ($100,000 divided by .11) and $1 million ($100,000 divided by .10).

A one-hour discussion with a good appraiser will introduce you to his method of calculation. Suffice it to say here that the valuation will require that the appraiser make several assumptions, including:[25]

1.   current rental value of the property

2.   future rental value of the property

3.   current and future operating expenses

4.   vacancy rates

5.   residual value, which requires several assumptions about the future

6.   capitalization rate.

All of these assumptions are matters of opinion and are thus subject to discussion. Most good appraisers will listen to your views. All appraisers are anxious to establish good relationships with active real estate players.[26]

The point here is that you can often influence your appraisal—by means of (informed) discussion with your appraiser about methodology and assumptions—and thus the amount of financing available to you. The idea is to learn the appraiser's methods, speak with him both before and while he is doing the appraisal and give him as much information as you can to help him reach conclusions favorable to you. The objective is not to "buy" an appraisal, for good lenders are quite capable of identifying poor appraisals and appraisers, but rather to attempt to convince a good appraiser of the validity of your assumptions, by using hard, verifiable data and projections. The difference in result can be tremendous and thus well worth your while.

A short illustration will highlight the value of working hand in hand with your appraiser. Suppose you are going to renovate a 2,500 square foot office building. The purchase price is $200,000 and the projected renovation costs are $100,000. You would like to obtain as much financing as possible.

The lender tells you that he will lend you 80% of the value of the completed project as a construction loan, which he will then convert into a permanent loan upon completion of the renovation. The key is: what is the future value of the renovated project? Your appraiser will have to make a lot of assumptions, e.g., post-renovation rental value. If you can persuade him that the rental value is $2 to $3 per square foot more than he originally thought, you will have made a sizable impact on his final numbers. If he ordinarily would have come in with a $300,000 value, you would have been offered a $240,000 loan. However, if through your efforts he comes in at a $350,000 value, you will be offered a $280,000 loan.

Real estate players who consistently buy undervalued properties, or properties to be renovated or developed, rely heavily on their appraiser. These players learn the logic of appraising and speak with their appraiser throughout the appraisal process. The result is that these players consistently finance 90% to 100% (or more) of the cost of their deals.

Construction Budgets

Often, when a property is to be renovated or improved with new construction, a lender will want to see a breakdown of the construction budget, that is, the estimated cost of renovation or new construction. The purpose of this request is to decide how much construction money to give you. It also may relate to the amount of permanent financing to be made available to you, as some lenders consider the total cost of the project in determining the amount of their loan.[27] As with appraisals, construction budgets can vary. Although there are accepted per-square-foot standards within the industry for different types of new construction, you may wish to show your lender how your costs will exceed the standards[28] so as not to limit the amount of your financing. And in renovation there really are no standards. Suppose again that you have found a 2,500 square foot office building which needs to be renovated. You talk to three general contractors about renovation and you get estimates of $80,000, $100,000 and $120,000 respectively. Which one will you bring to your lender? Many players will use the $120,000 budget because it will increase the amount of their potential financing. They will then hire the $80,000 contractor.

Is this deceiving the lender? I don't believe so if you are up front with him about what you are doing. For example, you may explain to him that you obtained three estimates and that you are using the highest because renovation is tricky and can often involve unforeseen costs once the work begins. Therefore, to be on the safe side, you explain, you are estimating your costs using the highest bid, although you may hire one of the other contractors and set up the balance as a reserve or contingency fund. If your presentation makes sense, most lenders will accept it.

Construction Loans

Construction loan is the term generally used to describe any loan which funds the development, construction or renovation phase of a real estate project. These loans are usually short term, the expectation being that they will be replaced ("taken out") when the project is completed and leased.

An important aspect of construction loans is that many lenders are willing to lend 100% of projected construction costs, the logic being that the construction money will at the least increase the value of the real estate dollar for dollar such that the money loaned is well secured by the land and improvements to the real estate. And, in practice, some lenders will loan more than 100% of the construction costs, lending the owner in addition some amount against his land and development costs.

For example, suppose Jones owns a piece of land for which he obtained zoning approval to build a 10,000 square foot office building. Say that Jones' land cost $200,000 and that he spent $20,000[29] obtaining the zoning approval. Jones' construction budget is $800,000 and he contemplates another $75,000 in "soft" costs[30] and $75,000 in construction interest[31] before the project is completed and leased. Given these facts, it would not be unusual for a lender to offer Jones $800,000 as a construction loan. In addition, Jones has some good arguments for more than $800,000. First, he might contend that as the total *cost* of the project is $1,170,000, an 80% loan against total cost would be $936,000. Second, he might attempt to show the *value*[32] of the completed project to be, say, $1,500,000[33] through the use of an appraisal and market comparables. If successful in establishing this value, then Jones can argue for an 80% loan of $1,200,000—essentially "cashing out" of the deal.[34] Many construction lenders will be open-minded to these requests, perhaps basing their final decision as to the amount on other factors: Jones' reputation and experience; Jones' creditworthiness; general market conditions and demand for office space; profitability of the loan, its rate and point(s).

Construction loans are generally advanced in stages, that is, on some predetermined basis tied to the progress of the construction or renovation. A good real estate player will learn to use the "float" on these advances to his advantage. For example, suppose that a construction loan is to be advanced 1/3 when framing is completed, 1/3 when the building is closed in ("tight") and rough plumbing and electrical are in, and the final 1/3 when the building is completed and a certificate of occupancy is issued. The sophisticated player can schedule these advances and the payments to his contractor(s) such that he always has money in his pocket—pushing payments to the contractor(s) as far back as possible. Some players are so good at this "game"—I am not making a judgment as to the business ethics of this tactic—that in a successful project they make the final payments to the contractor(s) with money taken as security deposits from tenants moving into the completed building.

Finding Collateral

A good real estate player should know how to find collateral—wherever it exists—when necessary to help with financing.

Suppose Jones' present project requires a $200,000 loan but, on the numbers, only warrants a $150,000 loan. Before bringing in a partner (see "Partners" below) or walking away from the deal, Jones should be creative in attempting to find collateral against which a lender might loan. For example, he may take a hard look at any other property he owns in an attempt to find equity against which a lender might secure the additional $50,000.[35]   If Jones has other property, he should analyze it *creatively* to determine whether it might satisfy the lender's need for $50,000 of collateral. For example, Jones may have purchased a 5,000 square foot office building two years ago, which on first blush would appear to be financed to the hilt. Suppose that Jones inherited the leases on the building and that the leases have two years left to run. Also suppose (as is quite common) that the market rental price for this office space is now much higher than the rent being paid by Jones' tenants, let's say by $4/square foot (net of all expenses). Therefore, in two more years, and presuming he can lease the space, Jones' rent roll will increase by *at least* $20,000 per year. (An argument can be made that the market rent will be even higher in two more years.)

In my opinion, given these facts, Jones has a good argument that this future cash flow—only two years off—increases the value (equity) of his office building today, even if the building were appraised only two years ago when Jones purchased it. Jones might make this presentation to his lender: "Mr. Lender, if we were to use a cap rate of between .11 and .12, the added value to my building of the additional $20,000 cash flow is between $167,000 and $182,000. We know the space is very leasable and the only issue is when I get it back from the present tenants. I know this is getting a little mathematical, but there are accepted standards for calculating the present worth of these future values.[36] I've done the homework, which I'd be glad to show you, and the present worth is in the range of $150,000. I think you'll agree[37] that even without calculating in the market increase which will assuredly occur during the next two years,[38] this property has plenty of value to cover my need for $50,000 of collateral."

Another example may give you the inspiration to flex your own creative muscles. The first project that our company undertook was the renovation of a small abandoned building into four condominium units. We were being financed by Bank A, which had gone through all the usual calculations in determining the amount of the construction loan they would advance. One month into the project, when the units were being framed, we came across another building for sale which we considered an exceptional opportunity—if we could find the money to buy it. The problem was that we needed to act quickly and we were about $100,000 short. The only financeable asset we had was the condominium project under renovation, and we knew (we had already asked) that Bank A was not willing to increase its construction mortgage.

Then, one of us *created* this analysis: "In three more months the four condominium units will be finished and available for sale. If they sell at the projected prices, we should *conservatively*[39] net $150,000 from the sale of the units. Suppose we ask for a one-year loan of $100,000, to be secured by our projected profit (a form of equity) on the sale of the condominium units?"

Since we knew that Bank A would not increase its loan, we approached Bank B and made our presentation. Bank B agreed and loaned us $100,000—against *projected future* equity in four *barely-framed* condominium units. (Sometimes you can surprise even yourself.) By the way, the second building, for which we needed the $100,000, was a renovation/transformation-type project (see Chapter 1) which has earned our company several million dollars since it was purchased in 1980.

Your Lender

Developing the Relationship

As an active real estate player, you will have few "assets" more valuable to you than a good lender. If an individual with credibility (even better, power) in an active lending institution believes in you and gets behind you, you are well on your way to success. Therefore, it is extremely important to cultivate and develop a good relationship with an aggressive real estate lender.

Here's a suggested game plan:

Identify the active real estate lending institutions in your area

While, as a general proposition lenders want/need to loan money (as such is the essence of their business), it does you no good to attempt to develop a relationship with, for example, a conservative savings bank uncomfortable with commercial real estate deals. Ask around. Which lending institution(s) is financing most of the projects which are similar to what you want to do.

Find the right person(s) within the lending institution

Although it is often not clear which individuals are the key people in the bank, it is well worth your effort to try to find out. This doesn't mean that you must deal with the president of the bank. Many times young, intelligent, lower-level people (who may not even have a title) are influential and respected within the bank and thus can have great sway in getting you the loans you want—even if they don't have much individual lending authority. In addition, as your deals get larger, your loan requests will usually go to a committee of several people. Here is where your ally can be a tremendous force if respected and able to make a good presentation in your behalf.

The importance of identifying the right person to work with cannot be overstated. I have lost count of the number of times that I have seen someone waste time and money wining and dining an "Assistant Vice President" who:

- is afraid of making aggressive loans, or
- is not intelligent or curious enough to understand anything other than very simple real estate deals, or
- is not well respected by the real decision makers within the bank, or

- is not able to present a loan request in a cogent, persuasive fashion, or
- just wants to put in his time and doesn't really care about developing good lending/borrowing relationships for his employer, or
- is lazy.

The results of the "wining and dining" is a "friend" in the bank who will never be able to get you the loans you need.

Explain to your lender your business and game plan
A good lender, even though intelligent, may not have a working understanding of real estate. Ask for his time so that you can give him an overview as to what you are trying to accomplish. For example, if you want to renovate, educate him about your approach and its advantages. Once informed, this person will be better able to structure loans meeting your needs and present your loan requests to the "higher-ups" or loan committees. What's more, you may end up with more than a good lender—you may end up with a knowledgeable friend with whom you can brainstorm new ideas or who will refer you to potential deals.

Remember that the street goes both ways
Most good lenders are ambitious. Therefore, it is important for you to be sensitive to what you can do for your lender. (I am not talking about personal inducements of any sort; I believe that nothing is more overrated than the practice of gift giving and/or "wining and dining.") Needless to say, meeting all your loan obligations is number one. But in addition, you should discuss with your lender what else he would like to see from you—for example, a deposit relationship is very important to most bankers; referral of new customers is also usually important.

Sell yourself with your results
A little self-promotion never hurts; so if your projects work out as planned (or better), be sure your lender knows it. Take him to see the renovated building, the leased store, the painted house, whatever, but use the opportunity to promote

your acumen and follow through. You will find that each time you "deliver" your lender a completed project, as promised, you will ease the way for your next loan.[40]

The objective of the game plan is to achieve a relationship with an individual and a lending institution which is based on trust and confidence. Your efforts should be an attempt to change your lender's attitude from skepticism (which all lenders must adopt toward new borrowers) to excitement and optimism for you and your approach to real estate. The value of this type of lender relationship is almost un-quantifiable—remember the importance of financing to a real estate player!

Getting the Loan

Make your lender's job easy
When requesting a loan, offer to get your lender any and all factual information or documentation which he may desire. Once you know what he wants, get it to him as quickly as possible, with the requested information presented in a clear and simple fashion. In other words, make your lender's job easy.

As a rule, lenders are not highly paid and don't have much of a support staff. Good lenders are also generally busy lenders. So, do everything you can to move the loan process along. Also, by assisting your lender in accumulating relevant factual information, you have the opportunity to present the facts in the light most favorable to your loan request.

In sum, never drop the ball. It's hard enough to get the best loans possible. Never give the lender a reason to delay or deny your loan request.

Negotiation
Although you must always keep in mind the importance of maintaining a good relationship with your lender, you should also understand that loans, like anything else, are negotiable. Perhaps your first (and maybe only) experience to date with a real estate loan has been a residential mortgage against your personal residence. Generally these loans are

not negotiable and you probably accepted the terms of the loan as offered to you.[41] In contrast, commercial real estate loans are usually not "take it or leave it." Once you have established a relationship with a lender, don't be afraid to negotiate the amount or terms of the loan. You may find the lender willing to move on rate or points, for example, or willing to trade points for rate or amount. Profitability and risk are what is important to the lender; so long as he perceives your request as not unduly cutting into profitability or increasing risk, he may agree to your requested modifications. Again remember, however, your most valuable asset as a real estate player is your lender. Don't push too hard. Don't ask for too much. Have a sense of your lender's parameters for negotiation. Don't ask for more than he can reasonably give you. In sum, negotiate sensibly and always leave your lender happy and anxious to hear about your next deal.

Partners

Although not commonly perceived as such, taking partners is really a means of financing—a way of buying real estate with other people's money. In partnerships, as with loans, you pay for the use of the money. Whereas in loans this cost is interest, in partnerships the cost is some portion of the benefits of the ownership of the real estate. The analysis is the same, however: what is the price of buying with other people's money? Sometimes it will be better to own 100% of a property and (assuming you can) take a large mortgage (even with what may be a high interest rate). Other times it may be preferable to take a smaller mortgage, take partners and own some portion of the property, less than 100%.

In considering the formation of a real estate partnership, keep in mind one key factor working for you—commercial real estate is actually a *group* of benefits: cash flow, appreciation, equity accumulation, tax shelter. A well-conceived partnership can allocate each benefit separately, creating an investment vehicle in which each partner receives that item (or a greater percentage of that item) which is most important to him. For example, you may know people with large annual incomes but very few assets. Such individuals might be willing to invest with you, trading off cash flow for a greater percentage of the appreciation potential of the deal. Or, as was very common prior to the 1986 Tax Reform Act, many people were interested in real estate primarily for its tax shelter aspect: most commonly, the paper loss of depreciation against other types of income. While the new law certainly changes the shelter aspect of real estate loss, it does allow the use of passive (real estate) loss to offset passive income and so there will still be people interested in investing in deals which provide them with a disproportionately large amount of passive loss. We will discuss taxes in Chapter 5, but for now assume that any investment property will generate a "paper" expense (not requiring actual out-of-pocket expenditures) for tax purposes, what is known as depreciation, and that while this expense may have little or no value to one person (depending upon his passive income and tax liability), it may have considerable value to someone who needs to "shelter"[42] passive income.

The IRS permits a partnership to divide tax loss in a manner different from other partnership benefits when there is an economic logic to the disproportionate allocation (see Chapter 5). As an example, you may put together a partnership in which one partner puts up 99% of the money and receives 99% of the tax loss (which may have no value to you), with all other elements of ownership split 50/50. Such a partnership can allow you to acquire real estate and share in its cash flow, equity build-up (as the mortgage debt is repaid) and appreciation—without investing much or any of your own money—while giving your partner something of value to him (passive tax loss) which may have no immediate value to you.[43]

Let's analyze a deal. Suppose Jones has located a small office building which can be purchased for $300,000. Let's assume that for one reason or another Jones cannot or chooses not to aggressively finance the purchase and thus will obtain only a $225,000 mortgage.[44] Jones needs $75,000 to close and $10,000 for closing costs, a total of $85,000. Jones goes to see his friend Smith, who, Jones knows, has cash in the bank. Jones makes the following proposal to Smith: Smith puts up $85,000, for which he is entitled to 90% of the tax loss[45] and a "noncumulative but preferred" return of 8% on his $85,000 investment. Also, on sale or refinance, Smith gets his $85,000 out first and then any profit or refinance moneys will be divided equally.

Let's analyze this proposal both from Smith's and Jones' perspectives. First, what is a "noncumulative but preferred return"? It is a return which must be paid to Smith after operating expenses and mortgage payments are made but only if there is money left over. It is "noncumulative" in the sense that it is only paid if there is money available, and payments which the partnership misses because it does not have the money are not owed to Smith (if the agreed-to return was "cumulative," payments not made to Smith would be treated like accounts receivable which would have to be cleared up before Jones received any return). It is "preferred"[46] in the sense that after operating and mortgage payments, it is the first thing to be paid, and if there is only enough cash flow to pay Smith 8% on his $85,000, then Jones gets nothing.

Smith's Position

Today Smith can deposit his money in a bank money market account and earn (let's assume) 6%, or $5,100 per year. As Smith is in the 28% tax bracket, his after-tax return on the $85,000 is actually $3,672 ($5,100 × .28 = $1,428; $5,100 − $1,428 = $3,672). Should Smith accept Jones' proposal? (Some of the ensuing analysis deals with taxes, the concepts of which will be explained further in Chapter 5.)

What is the likelihood of Smith receiving the 8% cash return and when?

Since Smith's return is not guaranteed, Smith must consider whether he will ever see a return at all. Assume Smith analyzes the deal and concludes that after six months it will begin paying him the 8% return. Since it is noncumulative, Smith earns nothing for the first six months of the partnership but then earns $567/month, or $3,400 for the last six months of the first year of the partnership. Now how does the deal look? Smith will earn in the first year of the partnership $3,400 plus 90% of the tax loss generated from the property. What is the tax loss? Jones has represented to Smith that there will be no out-of-pocket loss from the property and that the only loss will be depreciation. As we will discuss in Chapter 5, only the building is depreciable and, assuming a value of $250,000 and using the new law's straight-line schedule of 31.5 years, the annual depreciation loss is $7,936. Smith's 90% share is thus $7,142. Since this loss will offset his first year's $3,400 of income, his 8% return that year is tax-free and he will still have $3,742 of loss remaining, which he can carry forward to future years (or use against other passive income he may have). Smith's after-tax cash return in year one ($3,400) is thus very close to what he earns by simply leaving his money in the bank ($3,672) and he still has other passive loss to use or carry forward plus other rights of real estate ownership (for example, 50% of the appreciation). And, assuming a return of 8% is paid to him every year after the first year, in the second year his cash return will be $6,800, which is all sheltered by his $7,142 of annual loss (leaving him $342 of additional loss), putting him in a much better position than if he left his money in the bank.

What is the likelihood of appreciation and profit on sale?

Smith reviews comparable properties and determines that the property should appreciate 6% per year. The partnership agreement provides that the property will be sold within five years, and so Smith calculates the value of the appreciation. At 6% per year (not compounded), the property would sell for $390,000 five years later ($300,000 × .06 = $18,000 × 5 = $90,000). After deducting closing costs, let's say the net sales price will be $360,000. Then the bank has to be paid, and, assuming the mortgage is interest only, $225,000 will go to the bank. The next $85,000 goes to Smith as repayment of his investment and the $50,000 balance will be split evenly between Smith and Jones. So, Smith stands to earn another $25,000. What is the tax impact of the sale?

First, Smith must "recapture" (pay taxes on—see Chapter 5) the five years of depreciation which he's already taken, in our example, $35,710 (5 × $7,142). Second, he must pay taxes on his $25,000 gain. As we know that Smith is in the 28% bracket, his potential tax liability on sale will be 28% of $60,710 ($25,000 + $35,710) or $16,998. But, as discussed, Smith had some loss in the first five years of the partnership which he was not able to use against cash flow (or, as the old law would have allowed, against other income). In year one this loss was $3,742, and in years two through five, the loss was $342 per year. Totaling these losses, Smith has $5,110 of loss to use against gain, reducing his taxable gain on sale to $55,600 ($60,710 − $5,110) and his tax liability to $15,568. So Smith's actual, after-tax profit on sale is $9,432 ($25,000 − $15,568). Dividing this profit by five (years) adds another $1,886 per year of after-tax cash return to Smith's investment.

Now let's analyze Smith's investment. Here's what Smith's five-year after-tax return looks like:

	Sheltered Cash Flow	Average After-Tax Gain on Sale
Year No. 1:	$ 3,400	$ 1,886
Year No. 2:	6,800	1,886
Year No. 3:	6,800	1,886
Year No. 4:	6,800	1,886
Year No. 5:	6,800	1,886
	$30,600	$ 9,430

This is a total five-year after-tax return of $40,030 or a five-year average of about $8,000 per year. Had Smith left his $85,000 in the bank, his after-tax return (assuming interest rates stayed constant) would have been $3,672 per year. Therefore, Jones' partnership proposal makes good sense to Smith.

Smith's analysis required that he do some homework to determine, for example, the likelihood of his receiving an 8% return and when. Smith may or may not feel comfortable doing this analysis, and a lack of confidence in his ability to answer this and other questions may deter him from making the investment. Thus, Jones' credibility becomes a key factor in his ability to raise money from prospective partners, even when the proposed partnership makes excellent economic sense. It is therefore critical for a beginning real estate player to establish early a good reputation for business judgment and integrity.

The real estate player who contemplates buying with partners, must establish credibility with wealthy individuals who are interested in investing in real estate. Once perceived as honest and a "winner," however, he will have an unlimited supply of partnership capital. Knowing that this money is available when he needs it, the player can negotiate deals aggressively, with confidence that there is plenty of cash[47] behind him.

The way to attain this type of credibility in the investing community may be commonsensical, but a few points are nevertheless worth listing:

1. Your general reputation for integrity is critical. Remember this in all your business dealings.
2. Once you conclude your first successful deal, be it on your own or with partners, promote your result. Without directly tooting your own horn, make sure the right people know about the deal; let them spread the word. Everyone wants to tie on with a winner and soon you will develop a following.
3. Do everything within your power to achieve a return for your partner which is at least (if not more than) what you represented it would be.[48] Real estate has an element of risk and you cannot always be right. But do not leave a stone unturned in the effort to attain or better your projections. You may even consider going into your own pocket to make good on your projections when the deal doesn't work as expected, for, if you take a long-term approach, you may conclude that the value of a strong following of investors far exceeds the cost of occasionally dipping into your own pocket.

Once your reputation is established, you will find dollars chasing you. Then you will be in the driver's seat both in terms of the aggressiveness you can take in locating and negotiating properties, and in the position you can take in structuring the deal between you and your prospective partner(s). What's more, once you earn a reputation as an honest and capable real estate player, people will invest in you, not in the deal. Instead of analyzing the deal, as Smith did above, people figure that if you like it, it must be good.

After a while people won't even listen to you when you try to explain to them the numbers, and they will stop asking you to convince their accountant, lawyer or adviser. While this position is a great advantage in terms of your growth as an active real estate player, it is also a tremendous responsibility which must be taken very seriously.

Jones' Position

We've already determined that the partnership makes sense for Smith but what about Jones? Jones' analysis is different from Smith's; Jones should ask himself the following questions:

Can he do the deal alone?
If Jones cannot pull the deal off with his own or borrowed funds, he has no choice but to take a partner.

If he can do the deal alone only by borrowing aggressively, should he?
If Jones doesn't have his own cash to use, he must borrow, in one form or another, 100% of the acquisition and closing costs. This financing may mean a heavy negative cash flow, which Jones may not be able to carry comfortably. This pressure may force Jones to compromise his game plan. For example, instead of holding out to get the right tenant or group of tenants, Jones may have to rent quickly in order to carry the property and the long-term results may be disastrous.[49]

Is he trading away something that he doesn't need anyway?
Jones must analyze his own needs for loss from the property before he trades away 90% of it to Smith, for (presumably) eventually the property will throw cash flow or gain on sales to Jones—which he will want to shelter. Perhaps Jones' analysis is that he won't see much cash flow for several years (remember, Smith has first "dibs" on cash flow until he is receiving a return of 8% on his investment) and that by the time of sale (five years later) and given a maximum rate of 28%, it's better for him to buy with Smith's money, trade off 90% of the tax loss, and worry about the taxes due on his gain

(remember, without Smith's $85,000 Jones might not have seen *any* gain) in five years.

Can he set up the deal such that he puts money in his pocket and still owns a good piece of the real estate?

Some players will finance a deal 100% and still take partners—putting the partnership investment into their pockets. So long as the projected return to the partners is competitive and their funds are not at unreasonable risk, the partners shouldn't care that the player puts money in his pocket. And what's more, this money may be "tax-free" to the player since it is reflected in his partnership account (which must "repay" the partnership on sale or refinance), and therefore may be considered nontaxable debt (see Chapter 5). Accordingly, the player can end up with "tax-free" money in his pocket and a good-sized "back-end"[50] piece of the real estate—a nice setup if you can get it.

In our example, we don't have enough information about Jones to know whether he is doing the right thing by forming a partnership with Smith. Perhaps he's doing it for one or more *noneconomic* reasons:

1. Two heads are better than one. Perhaps Jones feels that Smith's business experience and/or contacts will bring something to the partnership. Maybe Jones feels that synergy will apply, that the business ability and judgment of the whole will be greater than the sum of the individual parts.
2. To share the worries. Most people handle risk better when they're sharing it with someone else. The feeling of "going it alone" is very difficult for some people, most of whom function much better knowing they have a partner(s) to help them deal with the possibility of crisis.
3. To establish a network of partnership capital. Perhaps Jones has no need for Smith's money on this project but feels that his growth as a real estate player depends on his increasing sources of investor capital. Maybe Jones feels that by making Smith (who has many wealthy friends) happy, he will open doors to additional partnership capital.

4.   Diminishing financial reward—doing deals for other reasons. Jones may feel that the partnership with Smith will simply be a lot of fun. While doing real estate deals with friends and/or family can be hazardous, it can, on occasion, also lead to great and lasting partnerships/friendships, for when it works, a partnership with a friend can be great: "the joy of victory" (and even the agony of defeat) is often twice as enjoyable (or one half as difficult) when shared with a friend. The idea of forming a partnership for fun—when hard dollars are on the line—may seem strange to the beginning (and perhaps struggling) entrepreneur/real estate player. But one's priorities can change once a certain level of financial success has been achieved. In my opinion, there is a point of financial security above which every additional dollar has a diminished significance to the recipient.

While some people may like the feeling of more money in the bank, I believe that many real estate players who attain a certain level of wealth lose interest in the money per se. In my opinion, these financially independent players continue to play the game as much for the game—the challenge, the personal interactions, the competition—as for the prospect of making additional bucks.[51] True, money is still very important, but in large part because it's the game's barometer of success or failure—essentially one's report card. These are my opinions and I have no way of documenting or confirming them. But, ask around. Speak with any real estate players you know. If I am right, it's a great recommendation for the game, for it means that while many real estate players no longer need to "work," they continue to "slug it out" merely for the enjoyment of the game. I suggest that this is the kind of "work" you want to get into!

Types of Partnerships

If you decide to form a partnership you have two choices:

General Partnership
In a general partnership each partner is liable for the debts and obligations of the partnership entity. Although a creditor

can only collect once on a debt, he can collect the entire debt from any one of the partners, that is, the creditor need not divide the debt among the partners and collect a proportional share from each. Each partner must therefore ask himself to what extent the risks of ownership of the real estate are covered, and similarly what his individual exposure is.

The most obvious partnership debt is the mortgage and each partner must analyze the risk of a deficiency action (assuming the mortgage is recourse and the state in which the property is located permits deficiency actions). Will the existent and/or projected gross rents from the property cover the operating expenses and debt service? If not, for how long can the partnership cover the negative cash flow and what is the risk of foreclosure? If the partnership does get into financial difficulty, can the property be sold, and for how much? In considering the partnership's financial strength and the possibility of a deficiency action, each partner should be aware of the financial condition of his partner(s). In the event that there are financial difficulties, can the other partner(s) come up with his share of the money to cover the negative cash flow and carry the property? In the event of a foreclosure and a deficiency action, who will the mortgagee go after? If your partner(s) has no assets or assets that are illiquid and/or nonsecurable, you can expect to be the one that the mortgagee will chase.

The point is that if you are one of a partnership and you are the one bringing the good credit to the party, be aware of it. That credit may be a very important ingredient in obtaining the financing for purchase and, in that regard, you are probably taking a disproportionate amount of risk, since you are the most likely target in the event of a problem. By being aware of this fact, you should be able to negotiate a better partnership deal for yourself.

Besides mortgage debt, what are the other risks to a general partner of real estate ownership? Another area of potential liability is the risk of someone being hurt on the partnership property. The partnership is not responsible for any injury; the injured party must generally establish that the accident occurred due to the "negligence" of the property owner. What is negligence? Theoretically, it is action or inaction of a property owner which falls below the standard of a "reasonable property owner." For example, if a reasonable property owner would have lights in his parking lot and you do not, someone (authorized to be on your property[52]) who trips in your lot at night and hurts himself will allege your negligence in not having put lights in the parking lot.[53] In practice, negligence is any action or inaction which a creative plaintiff's attorney can utilize in convincing a judge and/or jury to award an injured party a payment of your money. The only answer: plenty of insurance. Therefore, be sure that the partnership is adequately insured, and that if your insurer examines the property and identifies potential problem areas to be corrected or repaired, be sure that the work is done immediately and properly.

I also suggest that your leases contain plenty of exculpatory language[54] (with which a good real estate attorney should be familiar), for another area of potential liability is tenant lawsuits, not all of which are insurable.[55] The objective is to attempt to "contract away" these types of claims with a good "landlord's lease."[56] Other ways landlords protect themselves: (a) hold title in a noncredit entity, such as a limited partnership with a "strawman" general partner; (b) insert limited liability clauses in the Lease, such as: "Notwithstanding anything herein to the contrary, in the event of any liability from Landlord to Tenant, Tenant's only recourse shall be against Landlord's equity, if any, in the real estate of which the leased premises are a part, and Tenant agrees that in no event will it attach, encumber or in any way seek to enforce a judgment against other of the Landlord's assets."

One other risk to consider: as a general partner you are liable for the actions of the partnership entity. Therefore, anything done by your partner(s) within the scope of the partnership's activity could mean liability to you.[57] As an example, if your partner forgets to consult with you and contracts for a new roof to be put on the partnership real estate, this contract obligation, if not paid by the partnership, can probably be enforced against you.

The point is that as a general partner you are considered by the law an active player such that partnership liability can accrue to you. Therefore, you must be aware of the partnership risks and how each risk is limited and addressed.

One final point: you can see the importance of thoroughly checking your partners before entering a general partnership. Once again an earlier lesson repeats itself: the importance of operating honestly and maintaining a good reputation cannot be overstated. As a player who may someday want to raise money in the partnership format, you must operate in a 100% honorable and above-board manner. The result will be an unlimited supply of partners and partnership capital.

Limited Partnership[58]

In a limited partnership there is at least one general and one limited partner. (There can, of course, be several more of each.) The general partner is active in the operation and management of the real estate. He is what we have defined as a player. He is responsible for the debts of the partnership and makes all partnership decisions. The limited partner is a passive investor. He cannot be active in the management and decision making of the partnership, for if he is, he could legally be deemed a general partner. The limited partner is not liable for partnership debts[59] and his only exposure is the amount of his partnership investment.

A limited partner, acts merely as a passive investor and not as a real estate player; accordingly, he does not earn a return tied to his efforts (as does the player). He is just a money man and his return is commensurate with this position.

Any general partner is going to structure a return to the limited partner based on other returns available in the market place to an individual who wants a limited-risk investment. The general partner will be aware of the going rates for money market accounts, certificates of deposit, municipal bonds, etc. and will "price his deal" accordingly—that is, offer to the prospective limited partner an after-tax return higher[60] than that available from these instruments, *but* only high enough to attract limited partnership capital. In sum the limited partner rarely stands to make the kind of return that a real estate player (general partner) can make by structuring, creating and developing a deal from scratch.

The real estate player who wants/needs partnership capital may choose to form a limited partnership and act as the general partner for any of several reasons:

1. He wants to be the only decision maker.

2. He feels that it is easier to raise money when his prospective investors (the limited partners) have a limited risk.

3. He can cut a better partnership deal for himself, the general partner, if all other partners besides him have a defined risk.

Syndication

Syndication is basically the bringing together of a group of investors to undertake a real estate deal. Syndication of real estate has been a big business in the United States and the larger syndicators raise hundreds of millions of dollars every year; this industry is now in a state of great flux, however, as the 1986 Tax Reform Act has negated one of the syndicator's most important tools—the transfer of tax loss to shelter non-real-estate related income or gain. The usual vehicle for ownership is the limited partnership, with the syndicator or an entity which it controls acting as the general partner. The investors are the limited partners.

Syndicators, as such, are arguably not real estate players in that most of them make their money primarily from up-front fees and back-end pieces of the real estate which the syndicate purchases.[61] Their business is usually not the creation of value by means of an active revitalization or development of the real estate. As such, they are not really participating in what I've termed the real estate game.

The real estate player who wants to raise partnership capital is "syndicating" (raising money to form an investment group) even though the act of raising money is not the thrust of his business. Therefore, he should be generally familiar with the laws regulating the sale of partnership interests, or "securities."

Federal laws prescribe certain registration requirements which are quite burdensome and which generally only apply to large real estate syndications.[62] The federal laws also contain several disclosure and antifraud provisions which apply to anyone selling "security" interests. A new federal law requires that certain tax shelter deals be identified to the Internal Revenue Service. The intent of the law is to help the I.R.S. curb abuses; the fear is that the identification procedure will scare off potential investors in any offering which must be registered with the I.R.S.

Every state also has laws regulating the sale of securities, known generally as "blue-sky" laws. They are similar to the federal laws.

The aim of the federal and state laws is the prevention of misrepresentation and/or nondisclosure in the offering or sale of securities. These laws can be quite complex and confusing but generally only require preoffering registration and approval for very large deals. Still, if raising partnership money is to be an important part of your real estate game plan, you should consult with an attorney and/or educate yourself about the general provisions of the federal and state laws pertaining to the sale of partnership interests.

Notes to Chapter 3

1.   Divide the amount of the loan by the number of years of the loan to determine the annual principal payment.

2.   Interest payments will decline every year because they are calculated on the principal balance outstanding, which decreases every year.

3.   Gross rental minus all operating expenses, or the rental (net) available to service the debt.

4.   In analyzing "negative cash flow," you must consider how much of it is debt reduction (here $9,000/year went to debt reduction), because that amount is really not a loss in that it's reducing the amount of money owed.

5. That portion which represents debt is not deductible; In the $90,000 loan example, Smith actually has a taxable gain of $7,150. Smith must also be wary of a situation where he has "taxable income" ($7,150 in the example) *but* no cash (the example shows a *negative* cash flow) to pay his taxes. Presumably depreciation (discussed in Chapter 5) will solve some or all of Smith's problems.

6. These loans are still available for owner-occupied residential mortgages.

7. The word "point" is used frequently in the real estate game but it always means 1% of something. For example, a "two point" origination fee means that the borrower pays two percent of the loan amount as a fee for obtaining the loan. (A two point origination fee on a $250,000 loan would thus be $5,000.) Or, a loan which floats "three points" over prime means that the interest rate is three percentage points over the prime rate. (The prime rate today is 9.5%; thus an interest rate three points over prime is 12.5%.)

8. Depending upon the state and the type of loan, the lender may have grounds for a deficiency action (a lawsuit for the amount of his loan plus costs which he did not recover) against the borrower, but this action is only as good as the borrower's assets. I will discuss recourse and nonrecourse loans later in this chapter.

9. A "purchase-money mortgage" is an often-used term to describe seller financing.

10. In real estate terminology first mortgages are just called "firsts" and so on.

11. At this point, Seller has little choice but to execute the appropriate subordination documents—even if he is surprised by the amount of the first mortgage—for Buyer's mortgage has all the indicia of a construction mortgage (see the section on Construction Loans later in the chapter). The time for Seller to consider what Buyer might do is when Seller is asked to agree to subordinate to future financing—at the

negotiation stage. A sophisticated Seller would have put a dollar limit on the amount of the first mortgage. If the amount were to be *just* actual construction costs, he might talk to a contractor or architect to get his own rough estimate of the dollars involved. Alternatively, Seller might do a better job in negotiating the clause in his mortgage regarding future subordination. For example: "Mortgagee (Seller) agrees to execute whatever subordination documents are necessary to subordinate Seller's mortgage to a construction mortgage—so long as the amount of said construction mortgage does not exceed the Mortgagor's (Buyer's) actual projected out-of-pocket construction costs, as certified to by Mortgagor's architect." Now at least Seller has some review procedure over the amount of Buyer's first mortgage.

12. We'll discuss the tax treatment of overfinancing proceeds in Chapter 5. For now suffice it to say that debt proceeds are not "income" and thus not taxable.

13. In recent years, long-term lenders have been reluctant to make assumable and/or fixed-rate commercial loans. Thus, if you come across such a loan today, it probably dates back at least five years.

14. Buyer had no money, so he brought in a partner who put in the $100,000 cash. Basically the deal between Buyer and his partner was that the partner would be entitled to 90% of the tax loss on the building (as Buyer had no income, he didn't mind giving away the tax loss), that Buyer would manage the property (Buyer didn't have any money but he did have plenty of time and enthusiasm) and that upon sale Buyer and his partner would split the profits (after the partner got back his $100,000) 50-50.

15. Remember Seller's mortgage could now be subordinated to a $175,000 first mortgage ($100,000 plus three times $25,000) which was very easy to obtain with a $1,400,000 sales price.

16. Since Buyer 1 had a partner, Buyer 1's take was $3,444/ month.

17. Or, even better (from a lender's point of view) is the acceleration clause, language which accelerates the due date of the loan to the date of a "transfer" by the borrower of "any interest" in the mortgaged property.

18. There are some real risks to the buyer because he does not have legal title to the property until the end of the contract period.

19. There are risks to a seller whenever he "sells" (which for all intents and purposes he does when he enters an installment contract) and creates assumable financing without the lender's consent, for the seller is still liable on the underlying debt. If, as an example, the new "owner" of the property lets insurance coverage lapse and the building(s) on the property is destroyed and the original lender has to foreclose, the seller may have trouble. If the foreclosure proceeds are less than the outstanding debt and a deficiency judgment is possible, the seller may have to make up the difference.

20. Assuming an interest rate spread between Seller's existent loan and his loan to Buyer, there are several reasons why Seller may be able to keep his existent $500,000 first mortgage in place: the mortgage may be assumable anyway; the spread may be small enough that the lender doesn't care; Seller may be a very good customer of the lender; Seller may set up some mechanism to defeat the due-on-sale clause.

21. Seller is earning 2%, or $10,000, a year on the lender's money.

22. These procedures are to protect Jones: they prescribe the manner in which Smith must attempt to sell the house to prevent Smith from selling, for example, to the first bidder and then suing Jones for the difference.

23. Understanding how a lender evaluates and covers risk is important in structuring a prospective loan package, including a nonrecourse feature. For example, many lenders will decide how much they can *comfortably* advance against a

property by analyzing the ability of the property's income stream to cover the projected debt service. Essentially, the lender will identify the net operating income *and* then reduce it by some factor ("debt coverage ratio") which builds a risk protection into the loan. For example, suppose a property has a net operating income of $150,000/year. Many lenders will first deduct a vacancy and/or maintenance reserve—say, 3% ($4,500). This brings the lender's operating income figure to $145,500/year. Second, the lender will apply a debt coverage ratio, which is simply a reverse multiplier—a number which when divided into the operating income reduces it to the amount of operating income the lender wants available to service the debt. For example, if a lender wants operating income available in an amount equal to twice the projected debt service, then the debt coverage ratio is 2.0 (an unrealistically high figure), and he will divide the available operating income by 2.0. He will then loan an amount which can be serviced by the resultant figure, thereby insuring that the property generates twice the operating income necessary to service the loan. Most lenders use a debt coverage ratio of between 1.0 and 1.2. Assuming in our example that the lender uses 1.1, he will next divide $145,500 by 1.1, resulting in $132,272 of operating income with which the lender is comfortable in terms of servicing the debt. Third, in order to determine the amount he will advance, the lender will divide the resulting operating income by a percentage approximating the interest rate (and in some cases principal payments) he would expect to receive over the life of the loan. Let's say our lender uses 12.5%. This lender will thus loan $1,058,176 ($132,272 divided by .125) against this property on a recourse basis.

Now, back to nonrecourse. Suppose you say to this lender: "I understand why you want a recourse loan—simply to further insure your risk. Suppose we accomplish that objective in another manner—by increasing your debt coverage ratio. If you use a 1.2 debt coverage ratio the loan amount drops to $970,000 ($145,500 divided by 1.2 = $121,250 divided by .125 = $970,000) and since this amount reduces the possibility of the need for a deficiency action (and thus a recourse loan) your risk is well covered." Your lender may just accept this proposal and give you a nonrecourse $970,000 loan.

24. If you've analyzed the risk and, in your opinion, it is negligible, might it not be preferable for you to assume that risk rather than to pay (in one form or another) a nonrecourse lender for assuming that risk?

25. Some appraisers also calculate in the tax benefits of ownership (for example, depreciation and tax credits). Thus, the appraiser may need to be educated about the maximum tax benefits available from your project—even if he doesn't ask.

26. Most lenders will have an "approved list" of appraisers. It's a good idea to talk to a couple of the people on this list and select one who you believe will be the most likely to work with you.

27. A good appraisal can really help when the total cost of the project is well below the projected market value. You must attempt to persuade the lender that value is what he is loaning against—not cost.

28. So long as the difference makes for a better, more highly valued project. If you present a standard project with higher than standard expenses, your lender will assuredly be concerned.

29. Survey costs, legal fees, architectural fees, etc.

30. "Hard" costs are dollars spent on actual construction; "soft" costs are dollars spent on permits, legal and architectural fees, leasing commissions, and other nonconstruction expenditures.

31. Anyone undertaking a renovation or new construction project must remember to calculate into the total cost the estimated interest charges due on the construction loan during the period from the first "take-down" (first advance on the loan) until lease-up or "take-out" with a permanent loan.

32. Remember, it is always important for the player to distinguish between cost and value.

33. This is not an arbitrary figure, for given Jones' numbers, a completed value of $150 per square foot (in commercial real estate, analysis by square foot is very common) could be about right.

34. It would be very unlikely for a traditional construction lender to commit to $1,200,000 as a construction loan (when the total of hard and soft costs is $1,170,000), even if $1,500,000 is an accurate value of the completed project. While 100% of expected hard costs and some portion of soft costs is not an unusual construction loan, very few traditional construction lenders will advance against value. However, when dealing with a bank which makes both construction and take-out loans, a prospective borrower may get a construction loan the amount of which is based on eventual value and which is advanced in phases not just of construction but also of leasing. For example, Jones may get a loan commitment of $1,200,000 to be advanced $900,000 in stages as construction is completed; $150,000 when the building is 50% leased; and the balance when the building is 100% leased.

35. Other possibilities Jones should explore: convincing the lender to make an unsecured loan; bringing in a strong credit individual to cosign for the loan (in order to get an unsecured loan); offering the lender a non-real estate asset (e.g. car, stock, account receivables, etc.) as security for the loan.

36. See, for example, *Boston Financial Compound Interest and Annuity Tables* (Financial Publishing Company, 1979).

37. Always be confident, positive in approach and manner. "I think you'll agree" is much better than "Do you agree that...?" On the other hand, don't be too pushy or presumptuous: I prefer "I *think* you'll agree" to "I *know* you'll agree" or "You *can't* disagree that...."

38. I always like to end a pitch with something which makes my request seem eminently reasonable.

39. He was practicing his speech to the lender.

40. I have even seen real estate players pay off a loan sooner than promised (by refinancing with another lender, with the attendant costs of refinance) just for the purpose of generating good will and, whetting the (first) lender's appetite for the player's next deal.

41. The option with residential mortgages is usually not negotiation but rather shopping the different mortgage packages offered either from bank to bank or, even within one bank.

42. The common use of the word "shelter" derived from the fact that real estate losses (deductions) could, prior to the new law, offset or "shelter" taxable income and thus taxes due. The new law continues this offset, *but* only (with one exception, discussed below in Chapter 5) as to passive (which generally means real estate) income.

43. The new law does raise the question of how much loss you want to trade away, for loss may be carried into future years to offset your eventual (if everything goes well) cash flow or gain on sale.

44. For example, Jones may not be in a position to carry the building if it is 90% or 100% financed and it doesn't lease immediately. Or he may be a beginning real estate player who doesn't yet have a lender who will back him.

45. Remember that this allocation must have "economic effect," and when structuring such a partnership, Jones should speak with and obtain the assistance of a good accountant.

46. Since the return is only "preferred" and not "guaranteed," Jones is not personally obligated to pay the return.

47. "Cash" when used by a real estate player does not mean dollar bills. I am using it here to mean investment capital. It is

also often used to mean any funds other than assumed or seller financing; for example, you may offer a seller $250,000 "cash," meaning that he need not take back a mortgage, although you may 100% finance the purchase.

48. When dealing with prospective partners, our company tries to estimate projections conservatively, with the intention of delivering a return *better than* represented. Nothing makes an investor happier than getting more than he bargained for.

49. For example, Jones may be forced to take a tenant on a long-term, fixed-rent lease. This can be a real problem, for, as market rentals increase, the difference between market and lease rentals will have a negative effect on the value of a property subject to under-market rentals.

50. The term "back-end" is usually used to mean an ownership interest which is realized only after all mortgages are paid off and partnership capital returned.

51. My observation is that few real estate players stop playing once they achieve their financial objective. The fact is that the game is addictive.

52. In some states even a trespasser can sue you.

53. A good plaintiff's attorney will also allege negligence in that: (a) you allowed the condition over which his client tripped to exist; (b) your parking lot is not reasonably designed and laid out for safe passage; (c) etc., etc.

54. Language which absolves the landlord from liability. However, these clauses do not work in all situations and generally cannot shelter a landlord from negligence actions.

55. For example, a lawsuit by Tenant A against the landlord because noise generated within the building from Tenant B's business is impairing Tenant A's ability to do business. Basically, Tenant A alleges breach of lease protection of "quiet enjoyment," which is in almost every commercial lease.

56. For example, in the above situation, the landlord might have protected himself (assuming that Tenant B was already in the building prior to Tenant A signing a Lease) with a caluse such as: "Tenant has fully examined the Leased Premises, the Building, and the Common Areas and accepts same in all respects and enters this Lease at its own risk."

57. You are not responsible for actions of your partner(s) which have nothing to do with the partnership, such as reckless driving which leads to an injury. There could, however, be a problem if your partner's reckless driving occurred while he was doing partnership business.

58. Similar to the limited partnership is the ownership of real estate in the corporate form, in which the stockholders' exposure is limited to the corporate assets. But, the corporate form does not work for most real estate players for two reasons: (1) A corporation, as a separate legal entity, is taxed as it earns income—be it as cash flow or capital gain. Then, when the corporation attempts to pass money through to the owners (the shareholders), they, too, are taxed. This aspect of double taxation reduces the amount of after-tax income available from a real estate deal. (2) Although corporate losses can shelter corporate income, any additional loss must stay within the corporation and cannot be passed on to the shareholders. Therefore, in deals with limited cash flow and heavy depreciation, the depreciation loss would not accrue to the shareholders. Perhaps you are familiar with Subchapter S corporations which, although corporate entities, are taxed as partnerships, the taxable income and losses being passed directly to the shareholders without taxation at the corporate level. The problem with using a Subchapter S corporation to own real estate is that the tax losses available to a shareholder are strictly limited to not more than the amount the shareholder has at risk; in other words the "at-risk" rule (see Chapter 5) is applied to the stockholder's investment in the corporation, severely restricting the amount of tax loss which a shareholder is entitled to. The relative disadvantage of this situation may, however, change if the President's proposed

tax package is adopted (see introductory section of Chapter 5).

59. The prospective limited partner must check with his accountant as to the relationship between the amount he has at risk and the total amount of the real estate's tax loss available to him. The "at-risk" rule (which could change drastically if the President's tax package is adopted) as currently applied to a limited partner's investment in real estate says that the maximum amount of tax loss available to the limited partner (over the life of a real estate deal) is the limited partner's cash investment in the partnership plus his share (based on his percentage ownership of the partnership) of any partnership nonrecourse debt plus his share of any partnership recourse debt for which he personally signs. Accordingly, if the partnership is unable to obtain nonrecourse financing, then the limited partner must decide whether to limit his exposure on the mortgage debt (by not signing the recourse mortgage note) or, limit the amount of total tax loss available to him.

60. To account for the fact that an investment in real estate is less liquid and probably more risky than, for example, leaving the money in a money market account.

61. Most syndicators also manage the partnership real estate and thus earn a management fee.

62. The registration requirements need not be observed by "private" or intrastate offerings. Intrastate offerings involve situations in which the syndicator and all investors reside in the same state as the real estate. "Private" offerings are generally those limited by amount, number of investors, and type of investors. A player intending to raise partnership capital through what he believes to be a "private" offering should first consult a knowledgeable real estate attorney.

4

Contracts: Use Them to Your Advantage

The Key Elements of a Contract

A real estate sales contract is a legal agreement whereby one party agrees to buy and another agrees to sell a specific piece of real estate. It should be in writing and state at least:

- the parties
- the specific description of the real estate being transferred, including encumbrances (if any)
- the price and manner of payment
- the closing date and
- any contingencies to the seller's or buyer's obligations.

The presence of all five of these elements can sometimes be very important because of a law known as the Statute of Frauds.

The Statute of Frauds has been adopted in one form or another in all states and says, in sum, that any agreement to convey real estate must include all of the above elements, must be in writing, and must be signed by both parties. This requirement has been used by many a seller who has verbally agreed to sell his real estate and then changed his mind. It has also been used by the seller who scribbled on a piece of paper an intention to sell—which writing did not contain all of the foregoing five elements—and then backed off, arguing that as not all the elements of an agreement were in writing, the

Statute of Frauds prevented the writing from being an enforceable contract.

I learned about the Statute of Frauds the hard way. Soon after I had entered the real estate game, I became enthralled with a small apartment project. It had all the elements of what William Nickerson termed a "fixer-upper"[1] in his well-known book *How I Turned $1,000 into Three Million in Real Estate in My Spare Time*,[2] and I really wanted to buy it. I contacted the seller directly, and after several months of "thinking about it," he *verbally* agreed to sell me the property. We set up lunch to finalize our understanding, my intent being to come away from this meal with something in writing.

It was a very cordial meal and while I wanted to get something in writing, I didn't want to appear overanxious. We verbally agreed on all the basic elements of the deal and I decided to try for something in writing (and I wanted to get him to accept my check).[3] I knew that this seller was like a vulture and that if he smelled the blood of an overeager buyer the deal could change. So, in a very off-handed manner (trying to make it appear like an afterthought), I suggested that maybe we should scribble something down on a piece of scrap paper.[4]

The whole idea was so last minute and loose that he agreed and we wrote out the deal on a piece of scrap paper that both of us signed. He also took a check from me and I took our "agreement," promising to send him a copy as soon as I got back to my office. Driving away, I was quite proud of myself, for I had, after several months, finally convinced this very tough negotiator to sell to me at a price with which I was comfortable. Although this was one of my first deals, perhaps (I said to myself) I was just a quick starter!

A few days later I called the "seller" to talk about the deal and I was not a little taken back to hear: "What deal?"

I: "The deal we made at lunch last week."

He: "Oh that, I thought that was basically the opening of negotiations."

I: "What are you talking about? We've got a written contract."

He: "Yeah, well I asked my lawyer about that and he said that it didn't have enough of the elements of a contract to satisfy something called the Statute of Frauds and so wasn't enforceable."

I: (Losing confidence) "Yeah, well you also took my check."

He: (Gaining confidence) "Oh, I never cashed that—don't even know where it is."

I: Dial tone.

Needless to say, I was quite angry[5] and feeling that I was 100% in the right, I decided to sue. Just learning the game, I believed that a lawsuit would bring this man to his senses; I expected immediate capitulation. Soon I learned another valuable lesson.

I sued for specific performance, which is a request that the court order an owner to convey title according to a contract. The legal issue was whether our piece of scrap paper was an enforceable contract—that is, whether it contained enough of the critical elements of the deal to satisfy the Statute of Frauds.[6]

I was quite excited on the date the complaint was being served on the "seller," for I fully expected the "seller" to call me that very day to talk settlement. No call came. In fact, several months went by and there was no response other than his lawyer's routine filings, simply to avoid a default. The "seller" was boring me to death. I wanted action from the court system. I wanted the property! I was getting neither. Soon I called the "seller" and offered him more money. He counteroffered (asking for even more money) and we eventually settled and closed the deal. I had shown him!?

What did I learn from this experience? I learned about contract law—about the Statute of Frauds and stating each and every term of the deal in writing. I learned that the court system never works quickly and that if you go to court you have to be prepared to be patient and persistent. I also learned to read and control my own motivations. Why did I settle this matter—essentially give in to a dishonest seller—when I was convinced that I was in the right?

I was within the first few months of my commitment to the real estate game. I really wanted to get going and I thought this particular property was absolutely necessary to springboard me into the "big time." Even though I believed I was in the right and would eventually win in court, I couldn't wait. I wanted to sink my teeth into this property and turn it into a winner. So, I backed down and paid more money than I should have and more than the seller had already agreed to in writing.

Now, several years later, I can say that perhaps I did the right thing to settle, for this project gave me immediate visibility and credibility in the local real estate community. At the time, however, I just wanted action and probably acted a bit too quickly.[7] That is why, in addition to the lesson about the Statute of Frauds, I use the example to suggest the following:

- The court system rarely acts as a catharsis, a vent to the anger inside you. The courts can be quite ponderous and frustrating.[8]
- At all times, whether you are buying or selling, be in touch with what motivates you. In my case I paid more money for this property than I should have, primarily because I was impatient. I could barely wait to get to the plate, take my cuts, and swing for the long ball. While you may well sell or buy for noneconomic reasons, by being aware of your own motives, at least you will do so consciously, aware of your deviation from strict business judgment.
- In my opinion, there is no "one deal" which will determine your success (or not) as a real estate player. Part of my problem in the foregoing example was that I was reading that particular deal as critical to my advancement in the real estate game. This feeling, of course, contributed to my overanxiousness and thus willingness to overpay. It is true that there occasionally are "once in a lifetime" deals, and when they come along, you must do your best to tie them up. But these deals will only accelerate the process; sooner or later an intelligent and persistent approach to the real estate game will result in success.

The Legalese

In addition to the key elements of an agreement, the standard real estate contract contains a lot of legalese, which covers the following (among other things):

1. What happens if the seller can't deliver good or clear title (the legal documentation necessary to transfer legal ownership from one person to another) at closing?

2. What happens if the property is damaged between the date of contract and the date of closing?

3. What happens if the buyer can't close?

4. What representations does the seller make about the property (for example, with respect to zoning violations, encroachments, septic problems, etc.) and do they survive the closing?

5. In what condition must the property be delivered at closing?

6. What goes with the real estate (personal property)?

The beginning real estate player should obtain a standard contract and review it. He should get a feel for the way the contract addresses the above questions, as well as other matters pertaining to prospective transactions.

Using Contracts to Your Advantage

The good real estate player knows how to use a real estate contract to his advantage. The following examples are suggestions:

A Delayed Closing Date
with a "Stipulated Damages" Clause

Buyer has located a house for sale which Seller will sell for

$200,000. Buyer believes that the house is considerably undervalued, that its true value is $250,000 and that if he has enough time he can "flip"[10] the contract for $50,000. So Buyer offers to buy, with an immediate contract and 10% down, and so long as Seller agrees to a closing six months from the date of contract. Seller agrees. Buyer next instructs his lawyer that two other points, both fairly standard sales contract legalese, are critical to him: (1) the contract must stipulate that in the event Buyer can't close, Seller's only remedy is to keep Buyer's downpayment—in other words, Seller can't sue Buyer for breach of contract;[10] and (2) the contract must not contain a restriction on its assignment, that is, Buyer must be able to sell his right to buy at $200,000 to a third party.[11] Seller's attorney agrees.[12]

What Buyer has done is buy himself an option on Seller's house. As will be discussed in detail, an option is the right to buy real estate at an agreed price within an agreed period of time, the only consequence of a buyer's nonperformance being the forfeiture of the option amount, that is, the dollars which the buyer paid to obtain the option. For the price of $20,000 (10%),[13] which is all Buyer has at risk, he has six months to sell the contract at a profit.[14] Buyer has defined the maximum risk ($20,000) and concluded that the possible loss of this amount is worth the potential he has to make a profit within six months on resale of the contract. In our example, Buyer believes that there is a high probability that within six months he can sell the contract for a $50,000 profit and so he is willing to take what he perceives to be a very small risk (remember, in order to lose any money, Buyer has to be unable to sell the contract for $200,000 or more) of losing the $20,000.

The Use of Contingencies

A "contingency" is a defined event which must occur in order for one of the parties to a contract to be obligated to perform. Another way of saying the same thing: if the contingency does not occur, one of the parties (usually the buyer) can get out of the deal. A common example is a mortgage contingency which states: "The buyer's obligation hereunder is contingent upon his ability to obtain a mortgage of $X at an interest rate of Y% and for a term of Z years. In the event that the buyer is not able to obtain at least this mortgage by (date), then he must notify the seller in writing and the seller shall return the buyer's downpayment and the herein contract shall thereafter be null and void." In other words, the buyer's obligation under the contract only arises if he is able to obtain the described mortgage by the stated date.

It is through the use of contingencies that I have seen many examples of one party obtaining a distinct advantage over the other. Usually the scenario is that a creative buyer gets the seller to agree to an unrealistic (in practice, although not on its face) contingency and the contract thus becomes a totally one-sided (lopsided) agreement. In effect, the buyer creates an option *at no cost to himself.*

If the contingency is not realistically attainable by the buyer, then he controls the deal from the date of contract to the contingency date. For example, suppose the seller is unfamiliar with currently available commercial mortgages and agrees to a mortgage contingency, the terms of which mortgage just aren't available.[15] Now the buyer has a free ride, for he knows that he cannot obtain the defined mortgage and thus can play with the deal until the contingency date. During this period he can, among other things:

1. attempt to flip the contract, or

2. attempt to get 100% financing (very few sellers would agree to this contingency), or

3. attempt to find a money partner, or

4. attempt to find a tenant, or

5. attempt to get a reading on some zoning issue, or

6. etc., etc.

The point here is that the buyer is using the contingency to attempt to score on another's property, and yet has no downside, for if the buyer doesn't get what he needs, he can claim the contingency did not occur, back out of the deal and get his downpayment back. This type of one-sided situation is exactly what occurs when an *option* (discussed later) is negotiated; what is happening here, however, is that the sophisticated buyer is outwitting the less knowledgeable seller and essentially obtaining an option *for free*. (As we will see, when an option has been agreed to the seller gets paid for the buyer's "use" of the property in the event the buyer doesn't close.)

There are many examples of how a player can use a contingeny to his advantage and obtain many months of free time to play with a seller's real estate. The common denominator in each case is an unrealistic contingency, or a contingency which is realistic but over which the buyer has a great degree of control. The situation almost always arises when there is a difference in sophistication and knowledge between the buyer and the seller.[16]

Other common examples of this situation are zoning contingencies. For example, I have seen buyers convince sellers to enter contracts subject to the following types of contingencies:

1.   the buyer getting land subdivided into four lots,

2.   the buyer getting land approved for a 5,000 square foot office building,

3.   the buyer getting approval(s) for a 1,000 square foot addition to a building,

4.   the buyer getting a variance permitting five spaces of additional parking.

Note that in each case the buyer has stipulated a *specific number*—be it lots, square footage or parking spaces. In each case the creative buyer knows what is probably attainable and has established a number slightly higher—but not to the point of making the contingency appear unrealistic on its face. The seller may feel, for example, that the buyer should easily get approval for a 1,000 square foot addition to his building because neighboring lots of similar size have much larger buildings than his. But the seller may not be aware of recent changes to the local zoning code—of which the buyer is aware—making approval of the 1,000 square foot addition a real issue. And because the 1,000 square foot addition is a real issue and difficult to obtain, its achievement is probably within the buyer's control. Given this information gap, the buyer can create a one-sided contract and "use" the seller's property free of charge for a period of time. For example:

1. The buyer may apply for the 1,000 square foot addition in such a way that the result will probably be an approval *but* for slightly less than 1,000 square feet. He now knows that he has a free option[17] on the seller's property and can play with the deal (for example, attempt to get a tenant) for a certain period of time (until the contingency is up), knowing that if he is unsuccessful he can pull out of the deal.

2. He can submit a creative application to the zoning board asking for a 2,000 square foot addition, which in his opinion the board must either grant or reduce and approve as a 500 square foot addition. In this way, he is taking a flier on the seller's property—attempting to get twice what he and the seller discussed—knowing that he can back out of the deal if he doesn't get the 2,000 square foot approval.[18]

3. The buyer may have every intention of buying at the contract price even if the application for the addition is denied. Instead his game plan may be to use the contingency to delay the closing date as much as possible so that he can: (a) take advantage of appreciation between the date of contract and the date of closing and/or (b) attempt to find a tenant. For example, the contingency may read: "The buyer's obligation hereunder is contingent upon his obtaining zoning approval for a 1,000

square foot addition to the building. In no event may the buyer apply to the Zoning Board more than twice. The buyer agrees to submit his initial application on or before January 1, 1986 and in the event of a denial, his second application no more than thirty days thereafter." The seller may be comfortable with this time frame, believing that the contingency will be resolved one way or another within three to four months. But the knowledgeable buyer may know better, for he is aware of the zoning board's backlog and such that the period of time from the submission of his initial application (January 1, 1986) to a decision on his second application could be six to nine months. This buyer—not even caring whether he gets approval for the addition[19]—wants to buy right from the start. But he relies on the contingency (by making sure that his first application is unsuccessful) to delay the closing, using the delay to his advantage.

Options and Rights of First Refusal

Options

An option is an agreement whereby a prospective buyer pays an owner a certain amount of money and in return receives the owner's agreement to sell his real estate at a set price up to a stated date. If the buyer eventually buys, the option money is (usually) applied toward the purchase price; if the buyer does not proceed, the owner retains the money and the agreement expires. The advantage to a prospective buyer of obtaining an option is that it allows him to tie up a piece of real estate for a definite period and price, with the only exposure being his option money.

In my opinion, options are a very important tool for the real estate player (from the beginner to the sophisticated developer) for several reasons:

Analysis
As the deals you attempt get more complex, you will need

more time just to analyze them properly. Everything from market conditions to zoning laws and practices must be considered. But why not do this before making a financial commitment to the owner? Because many times a good piece of real estate is "hot"—there is a lot of buyer interest in it—and you may correctly assume that it will be gone within a couple of weeks. The option agreement is like a reservation—it saves the deal for you until you have had a chance to analyze it properly. And, generally you can limit your risk (if you can conclude your analysis quickly) as there is (usually) a direct relationship between the option period and the option money. For example, if you feel that you can analyze a deal within two weeks to a month, you should be able to obtain an option (unless it's a very large or very hot property) for $5,000 to $10,000.

Assemblage

You may be trying to assemble several pieces of property in order to create a site which has great value to you, and it is very possible that without the whole, the individual pieces may be of little value to you. Accordingly, whereas it may not make sense *to buy* any of the lots at the beginning of your attempt, you may be quite willing to option individual pieces. In this way, you can limit your risk, for in the event you cannot acquire all the parts that you need to create the whole, the worst case is that you forfeit your option money (which may be less expensive than attempting to resell pieces of land you've purchased).

Zoning

A common play with an option is to use the time you've purchased (the option period) in an attempt to get zoning approval for the development of the optioned property. For example, our company recently optioned a piece of land on which we hoped to build a 20,000 square foot office building. With the requisite zoning approval the land had considerable value to us; without the approval we didn't want the land. So, we entered an option agreement with the owner paying him the sum of $25,000 for his agreement to sell us his land at a set price so long as we closed within a nine-month period. In the event we closed, the $25,000 was to be applied to the purchase price; if we didn't close, the agreement was dead and the $25,000 was his.

We immediately applied for the zoning approval which we received within four or five months. We then obtained financing and closed within the nine-month option period. Although we could have lost the $25,000 (plus the costs of the zoning application—architectural plans, surveys, legal, application fees, traffic studies, etc.), we considered that possibility a more acceptable risk than buying the land outright—without knowing what we could build on it.

Going for the Long Ball

Occasionally you'll come across a piece of real estate which really intrigues you. You may, for example, conceive of a creative way to acquire the property or an exciting new approach to operating or marketing the property. But your idea may be a long shot and so you may be unwilling to take the risk of a standard contract or outright acquisition in order to test the validity of your idea. Here is where the option can be very useful.

If you can convince the owner to sell you an option, you can limit your risk while tying up the property. During the option period you can attempt to test your idea and subsequently (at the end of the option period) make a more informed judgment as to whether your concept—and thus purchase—makes sense.

I can give you an example of the long-ball approach which was used by my company several years ago. We had learned of a large (180,000 square foot) factory building which was for sale and which although very well located, was a "white elephant" in that no one really knew what to do with it. There was a retail tenant (a low-end discounter) occupying about half the building with a lease which ran for another 10 years. And, while the owner was willing to sell the building for $1,600,000 and take back a $1,100,000 purchase-money mortgage, the price was excessive in light of the low-rent, 10-

year lease to which the new owner would be subject—a lease which scared off the traditional (numbers-oriented) investors.

In visiting the building our little group came up with a "crazy" approach to the deal; the conversation went some thing like this:

Adams:	"The seller's offer of $1,100,000 of purchase-money financing is very exciting but where are we ever going to come up with the additional $500,000 necessary to close?"
Jones:	"Let's try to analyze this deal in a way nobody else has—maybe we'll come up with some ideas."[20]
Smith:	"Yes. Let's think about this tenant. All the other potential buyers are scared off because of the low-rent, 10-year lease, yet I have a feeling that nobody has asked the tenant if they even want to stay. Maybe they want out."
Jones:	"It's possible. They don't appear to be doing that well."
Adams:	"Hey. Maybe, if we bluff like we're long-term investors and are happy with the 10-year lease, they'll buy out of the lease!"
Jones and Smith:	"You're crazy!"
Smith:	"And even assuming we got them out, one, where do we get the $500,000 to close the deal, and two, then what do we do with this gigantic *empty* building?"
Jones:	"Yeah, well I was thinking about that. I think that this property would be a great location for a factory-outlet shopping center."

Smith and Adams:	"What's a factory-outlet shopping center?"
Jones:	"I'm not sure."

From this brainstorming session we went out and did some preliminary homework and decided that while our thoughts weren't crazy, they certainly were long shots. Nevertheless, we decided that it would be worth it to risk some money and test our ideas. So, we approached the owner and after some time were able to convince him to sell us for $25,000 (which we borrowed) a 90-day option on the property.[21] The agreed price was $1,600,000 with the seller taking back a purchase-money first mortgage of $1,100,000.

Then we scrambled, trying to use our 90 days as effectively as possible. We set up meetings with the tenant, we visited factory outlets, we researched the conversion to and usage of the factory building as a retail mall.

Ninety days later we were ready for closing. The tenant—much to our surprise (nobody had ever asked the tenant) had agreed to *buy out* of the lease—to *pay us* (once we got title) to terminate the 10-year lease obligation. The termination fee was $500,000: a $200,000 cash payment and a $300,000 low-interest loan to us (to be secured by a second mortgage behind the seller's first). With this agreement in writing we went cold to a bank[22] and asked for a loan of $500,000 *for a couple of hours*. Needless to say we had to explain the deal.

We described how we could buy the property for $1,600,000—$1,100,000 from a purchase-money mortgage and the balance, $500,000 with the bank's loan. We showed the banker a lease termination agreement (previously signed by us and the tenant) providing that a $500,000 termination fee (which was being held in escrow) would be paid to us immediately upon: (1) our displaying to the escrow agent a deed to us of the property and, (2) our executing a note[23] and mortgage deed for $300,000 (the portion of the termination fee which was a loan). So, we explained to the banker, all we needed was a $500,000 loan for a couple hours so that we could buy the property, display the deed to the escrow agent, and get the tenant's $500,000 termination fee. Fortunately for us we had found an open-minded, intelligent banker who listened carefully and then approved our loan.

At the closing, the bank's lawyer arrived with a check for $500,000 and the transaction went like this:

1. Bank loans us $500,000 (and we sign a promissory note), which we hand to seller.

2. We execute the $1,100,000 purchase-money note and mortgage deed to the seller.

3. Seller hands us the deed to the property.

4. Bank's lawyer takes the deed out of my hand.

5. Bank's lawyer goes into the next room and displays to the escrow agent the deed into us. We sign the $300,000 note and second mortgage deed to the tenant and the Lease Termination Agreement is released from escrow.

6. Escrow agent hands us the $500,000 check.

7. Bank's lawyer takes the check and tears up our promissory note to the bank.

8. We pay the bank one day's interest on the $500,000.

9. Everybody shakes hands.

What had started out as a "crazy" idea as to how we might acquire this property had become a reality. We had accomplished the purchase without any of our own money (or credit) and were now the proud owners of a 180,000 square foot factory building.

Our research into factory outlets was also productive. As it happened, the location was excellent for an outlet mall and by the time we closed, we had several interested tenants. This property has since become one of the most successful factory outlet malls in the country, now renting at a price per square foot well in excess of the purchase price (per square foot).

There are two points to the story:

1.   Options can be just the right tool for some deals. Here the option allowed us to tie up the property for 90 days, while risking only $25,000, in order to test a "far-fetched" approach to purchase and revitalization. In this situation, the long shot came in and we were able to turn our $25,000 flier into a highly successful real estate deal.

2.   Always try to break from the crowd in your approach to a difficult or unusual deal. Discipline yourself to think creatively—always looking for the angle nobody else has considered. While only one out of 50 ideas may pan out, when you "hit," it's well worth the effort!

Rights of First Refusal

A right of first refusal is an agreement by an owner of real estate giving another person the last word on the purchase of the owner's real estate. A typical right of first refusal given to say a Mr. Smith might read:

"Owner may not sell his real estate without first following the herein procedure: In the event Owner receives a bona fide written offer to purchase his real estate, which offer Owner is willing to accept, he shall notify Mr. Smith of said offer by delivering a copy thereof to Mr. Smith. Mr. Smith shall then have a period of 10 days in which to match said offer. In the event that Mr. Smith submits to Owner an identical written offer on or before the expiration of said 10-day period, then Owner must sell said real estate to Mr. Smith pursuant to the terms of said offer and so long as Mr. Smith acts within a reasonable period thereafter to enter a contract and close the purchase."

The right of first refusal should be in some document which is recorded on the land records. This protects the owner of the right of first refusal (Smith in the above example) from a situation in which the owner of the real estate either mistakenly or intentionally forgets about the right and sells his property to someone else, whose claim to the real estate (assuming that he purchased in good faith) will prevail over the owner of the *unrecorded* right of first refusal.[24]

Although rights of first refusal may seem relatively harmless, they can be very valuable things to own. For example, in discussing options we saw that in some situations a prospective buyer will attempt to purchase an option just for the opportunity to freely analyze a deal, without the fear of another buyer stepping in and getting the deal first. If an optionee—the property owner is the optionor and the person acquiring the option is the optionee—is willing to pay for this opportunity, so as to preclude other potential buyers from tying up a property while he is doing his analysis, won't a person in the optionee's position pay for a right of first refusal? In other words, won't that same person pay for the right to be the last one to analyze a deal, free of the fear that someone else can step in and buy the deal out from under him?

Our company was recently involved in an unusual situation which illustrates the value of rights of first refusal. A very well located building had just come on the market and we were interested in purchase. The building was 15,000 square feet (the first floor was occupied by a restaurant and the second floor by offices) and had all sorts of exciting renovation and leasing possibilities. This was just the kind of deal which excited us and we wanted to roll up our sleeves and really get into it. It was also a fairly complicated deal and we anticipated spending a lot of time conceptualizing the future use of the building, estimating the renovation costs, and analyzing the operating figures. Two other people were also interested in the property: another real estate player and, the owner of the restaurant on the first floor.

Soon after we learned about the availability of the real estate, we also learned that the owner of the restaurant had within his lease a right of first refusal on the real estate. This fact created a dilemma for us: should we even gear ourselves up, make an emotional commitment to the deal, invest time and money (architectural costs, building inspection, survey, etc.) and start negotiating with the owner of the real estate—knowing that at the end of all the analysis and negotiation the restaurant owner could conceivably step in, simply match our offer and take the deal? After considering both the upside on the deal (which we believed was considerable) and the likelihood of the restaurant owner exercising his right of first refusal, we decided to proceed. Presumably reaching a similar conclusion, the other real estate player interested in this property also began to actively analyze and pursue this deal.

After a relatively short but concentrated period of analysis and discussion, we were able to persuade the owner of the real estate to sell to us at a price of $1,500,000. I was pleased with this price as I believed that the property had a very good upside. At the same time, I was also worried that the restaurant owner, too, would like the price and exercise his right of first refusal. Soon there was an additional complicating factor.

The other real estate player began to offer the restaurant owner money to buy the right of first refusal.[25] Obviously he, too, had completed his analysis and concluded that $1,500,000 was a good price. Although the other game player offered to purchase the restaurant owner's right of first refusal for $100,000,[26] in the end the restaurant owner decided to exercise his right of first refusal and buy the real estate himself. If nothing else, this experience taught me that rights of first refusal can certainly have value.

What's interesting about rights of first refusal is that often they are acquired as incidental parts of another transaction. For example, the restaurant owner (perhaps as an afterthought while negotiating a lease) had asked for and received a right of first refusal. The lesson is that whenever negotiating for any interest in real estate (such as a lease of all or a major portion of a piece of property) always ask for a right of first refusal.[27] Unless the owner of the real estate is fairly sophisticated, you may well be able to convince him that all he's agreeing to is to give you the last crack at buying his property—if and when he decides to sell and at a price which he alone determines.[28] And you may end up with a very valuable right which is in reality a windfall to you since it is incidental to the specific real estate interest for which you were negotiating.

Leases

A lease is a contract in that it is an agreement between two parties, each having reciprocal rights and obligations. The knowledgeable real estate player knows that leases can be used in many different ways to create a successful real estate deal.

The Basics

The person with the immediate right to possession of the space being leased (as we will discuss shortly, this person is not always the owner of the real estate) is, of course, the "landlord," or "lessor," and the person obtaining the right to possession under the lease is the "tenant" or "lessee." The area being leased is generally described as the "leased premises" or "demised premises." The time period of the lease is the "lease term," usually starting on the "commencement date" and ending on the "termination date."

Key Elements in the Lease

Area of the Leased Premises

As most commercial leases are based on per square foot price, it is very important to identify the square foot area of the leased premises. Landlords tend to be very aggressive in this regard, generally measuring the gross area (including stairways, elevator shafts, common areas, mechanical rooms etc.), usually from the outside walls of the building containing the leased premises. Tenants try, whenever possible, to define the area of the leased premises as that portion of the square footage which they can actually use—that is, excluding from floor area any nonusable, or "dead," areas. The attempt to use common terminology for these areas yields phrases such as "gross," "rentable" and "usable" square footage.

If you are a landlord, you obviously want a very gross (large) measurement of floor area. When leasing smaller space, some landlords achieve higher-than-market per square foot rentals by not even mentioning square footage, instead displaying the premises to a prospective tenant and taking the position: "Here's the space we're renting—I need $1,000/month for it."[37] Many prospective tenants will accept this approach since at least they can see the actual area to be leased and can determine whether it's worth $1,000/month to them. From the landlord's point of view it's a great way to lease space at a higher-than-market rental. For example, if in the foregoing example the area being leased is 1,000 square feet and the market rent for similar space in town is $10/ square foot, simply by getting away from the square footage discussion, the landlord has achieved $12,000 rent/year, or $12/square foot—20% over market.

Rent

Needless to say, rent is a very critical term of any lease. Rent is paid in many different ways:

1. **Set Amount** In most residential leases (and some commercial leases) rent is often just a stipulated amount. Most apartments are simply displayed to a prospective tenant and the rent quoted as "$X per month"—usually, "plus utilities." There is generally no mention or consideration of square footage. Exceptions are expensive apartments in some metropolitan areas where the money at stake is so great that rent is in fact pegged to square footage.

2. **$ Per Square Foot** As mentioned, renting on the basis of the square footage of the leased premises is by far the most common method used in commercial leasing. Once the square footage is defined and the rent per square foot agreed upon, these two numbers are multiplied to get the annual rent. For example, if the leased premises is 5,500 square feet and the agreed per square foot rent is $17.50/square foot, then the annual rent is $96,250, or $8,020.83/month.

3. **Percentage Rent** Many retail leases contain percentage rent clauses. This rent is usually in addition to the rent per square foot or, "minimum" rent.[29]

Percentage rent is tied to a tenant's gross sales and is payable as some percentage of gross sales over a stated amount (sometimes termed the "break point"). For example, let's assume a tenant is leasing 2,500 square feet and the lease provides for $25,000/year of minimum rent (the tenant is paying $10/square foot) plus percentage rent of 5% (the specific percentage is a matter of negotiation, although the range is usually between 3% and 7%) of the tenant's annual gross sales over $500,000.[30] If the tenant's annual gross sales are $700,000 in the first year of the lease, then in that particular year the tenant will pay the landlord a total rent of $35,000—$25,000 of minimum rent plus 5% of gross sales over $500,000, or $10,000.

Percentage rent can be a great kicker for a landlord, but most landlords don't count on it until it's received. One reason is that the key factors leading to percentage rent—the gross sales of the retailer and the retailer's declaration of its gross sales—are 99% within the retailer's control. Nevertheless, I have seen smart tenants make an excellent rent deal for themselves by using a percentage rent pitch which puts stars in a landlord's eyes:

Retailer: "I'll do great things for your strip center. I'm a big advertiser and a great draw. Don't worry about my minimum rent because I'll be well past that with the percentage rent that I'll be paying you. I expect to do $1,000,000 in gross sales in year one. Come on—quit worrying."

The problem is that the landlord has less ability to estimate the tenant's projected gross sales than does the tenant. And if the tenant is not 100% honorable, the landlord will have a difficult time identifying the tenant's *actual* gross sales as opposed to the tenant's reported gross sales. The unsophisticated landlord might just hear from his tenant one year later:

Retailer: "Wow! Don't know what happened. I was sure I'd do a million dollars in sales. Must be the economy. Hey, like my new Cadillac?"

4. **Additional Charges** Rents are sometimes described as "gross," "net," "net net," or "net net net." These terms are very often confused and used differently in different parts of the country but the critical factor is always the same: what item, (if any), *in addition to rent,* is the tenant paying the landlord.[31] Tenants almost always pay their own utilities,

either directly to utility companies or to the landlord. What items the tenant pays in addition to utilities is up to the negotiation between the parties; these charges are often termed "additional rent."

A tenant must be careful that his landlord does not make a profit on the additional rent; some landlords make money on the additional charges by:

1. charging off as "operating costs of the real estate" improper items (such as the landlord's office expenses),

2. passing off capital improvements as maintenance charges,

3. collecting additional charges far in advance of when they are due and making money through the float on the tenant's money (the period of time that the landlord uses the tenant's money interest free),

4. allocating to several tenants within one building individual pro rata percentages for additional charges which total more then 100% of all charges, and/or

5. overstating actual charges.

The point is that as a tenant you should be aware of how a landlord can overcharge you for additional rent and protect against this possibility with a tight lease. As an example, a sophisticated tenant might require that the amount of the additional rent be stipulated in the lease, with maximum annual increases.

Making Money with Leases

The ownership of a leasehold interest can be the basis for a very successful real estate play. There are several ways to make money with leasehold interests:

"Ownership" without Cash or Financing
Sometimes the acquisition of long-term rights to posses-

sion by attaining a leasehold is preferable to outright purchase of the fee (or ownership) position.[32] The reason is that one acquires leasehold rights simply by signing a lease—there is usually no requirement of cash or financing (with the exception of a security deposit and/or advance rental payments). And, there are situations when a real estate player can sign a lease as a no-credit entity[33] such that he may not even have to put his credit on the line. The result can be the long-term control of real estate without cash, financing or credit.

Sublet and Assignment

One way to make money with a lease is to negotiate a favorable rental deal and then sublet or assign the lease rights or some portion thereof. In a "sublet" the tenant ("sublandlord") leases ("subleases") to another (the "subtenant") either a portion of the tenant's space or, some part of the time remaining in the lease term. In other words, the subtenant takes something less than all of the sublandlord's rights to possession. In an assignment, on the other hand, the tenant ("assignor") assigns its entire right under the lease—both in terms of area and time—to another (the "assignee"). In either case the tenant remains liable on the lease unless the landlord agrees to a release.[34]

The key to making money is, of course, buying low and selling high—subletting or assigning at rental rates in excess of the lease rentals. Or, with an assignment, a lease is often simply sold—the price representing the present value of the difference between the lease rental and the market value of the leased premises, multiplied by the time left to go on the lease. Many tenants have, in fact, signed leases at what were market rents and subsequently sold their leases for large profits (either to a third party or back to the landlord) when the appreciation in market rents exceeded the lease increases.

As an example, our company recently considered the purchasing of a lease of a 30,000 square foot building. The tenant was using about 7,500 square feet for himself; he had sublet the balance of the space on short-term subleases. The annual rental was $270,000 (triple net) or $9/square foot; the market rental for the space as of the date of our review was $20/square foot. The lease term (originally 30 years) had 19 years left with no increases in rental.

As the tenant's sublets were short term, we knew that we could have the entire building back and available to lease (sublease) within a year or two—a prospect of risk as well as opportunity. We decided that demand for the space would be high and so analyzed the purchase: if we could lease (sublease) the 30,000 square feet at $20/square foot (nnn), we would realize a triple net rental of $600,000/year. Deducting the rental obligation to the landlord of $270,000/year, our net income (before debt service on any money we borrowed to buy the lease) would be $330,000/year. The tenant wanted $2,500,000 for its lease[35] and so we had to analyze the present value of the income stream of $330,000 per year (which would increase[36] as market rates presumably continued to rise) over the next 17 to 18 years.[37] Using financial tables and an accepted (at the time) discount rate, we learned that the present value of the right to receive $330,000 per year for 17 years was roughly $2,000,000[38] and so we decided not to buy. The point is that substantial sums can be made by acquiring a long-term leasehold interest, the rental rates of which increase more slowly than market rents.

Master Leases—Buying Wholesale and Selling Retail

In some instances a game player might consider leasing a large area of space, then breaking it up and subleasing smaller areas. The idea would be to acquire a "master lease"[39] at wholesale rental rates and sublease the smaller spaces at retail rental rates.

A good example of this kind of use of a lease is the operation of the "office" or "executive suite" companies which have sprung up around the country. These companies master lease a block of space in an office building and then create many smaller individual offices within that area. Most of these companies also furnish the space, provide certain common areas (such as reception and conference rooms) and offer such services as phone answering and cleaning. The companies sublet these smaller offices to subtenants.[40]

The economics are these:[41] say that the master tenant (the owner of the master lease) leases 40,000 square feet in a new building at a market rent of $20/square foot,[42] for a total rent of $800,000 per year. The master tenant then spends $25/square foot to divide, finish and furnish the space, or a total of $1,000,000[43], which he borrows and repays over 20 years at interest and principal of, say $132,000/year.[44] In addition, let's say that the cost of providing a receptionist, (local) phone service and cleaning is $75,000/year and that marketing and administrative costs are $25,000/year. Therefore, the master tenant has a cost of operation of $1,032,000 per year ($800,000 rent plus $132,000 debt service plus $100,000 services).

Now let's assume that of the 40,000 square feet, 20% is either "core area"[45] or otherwise non-leaseable space (such as hallways). The balance, 32,000 square feet, is available to subdivide into smaller offices. If the average office is 200 square feet, the master tenant is able to create 160 offices. If these offices rent for an average of $750/month, the master tenant's gross monthly income is $120,000. Assuming a vacancy factor of 10%, the master tenant's monthly income before costs of operation is $108,000 month, or $1,296,000/year. Deducting the costs of operation, the master tenant's annual profit is about $264,000/year.

While some of this profit is made from the provision of services, the crux of the deal is the acquisition of space at $20/square foot and the subleasing of it at $45/square foot.[46] The point is that good money can be made by acquiring space at wholesale rentals, subdividing it, and then subleasing it at retail rentals.[47]

Protecting the Landlord's Interest

In most of the situations where an extraordinary profit is made from a leasehold interest, the landlord has neglected to adequately protect his interest. A sophisticated landlord, on the other hand, will employ a variety of techniques to protect against a tenant making a windfall profit on his lease.

Short Lease Terms

Rarely will a knowledgeable landlord (who is not in financial trouble) sign a long-term, fixed-rent lease. Some landlords won't even sign a lease with a term longer than three to five years although this policy can create marketing and financing problems. Nevertheless, I know of several very successful real estate players (landlords) who will sign only short-term leases, their philosophy being that desirable space will always lease and that by insuring its availability on the open market every three to five years, it will always yield the highest possible rent.

Consumer Price Index Increases

Most landlords will agree to leases longer than five years but only with rental adjustments. Depending on the deal negotiated between the landlord and tenant, these adjustments can occur every year to every five years.

Most adjustments are made according to the increase in the consumer price index from the date of the commencement of the lease (or the last adjustment date, as the case may be) to the present adjustment date. A typical clause might read: "The herein rental shall be adjusted every two years and shall be increased by the same percentage increase as occurred in the consumer price index from the commencement date of the lease (or the immediately preceding adjustment date) to the present adjustment date. As an example, if the consumer price index is 100 on the lease commencement date and 120 on the adjustment date, then the herein rent of $20,000/year shall be increased 20% to $24,000/year."

Restrictions on Sublet and Assignment

Some landlords attempt to prevent a tenant from realizing a profit on the landlord's real estate by restricting the tenant's ability to sublet the leased premises or, assign the lease without the landlord's consent. These restrictions are not solely intended to prevent the tenant from making a profit off the lease—all property owners want to know and have a say in who is occupying their property. But some landlords use (and sometimes manipulate) these restrictions to prevent *any* sublease or assignment whenever the space has become more valuable than the rental paid by the tenant.

A tenant can attempt to protect against unlimited landlord control by inserting a clause in the lease requiring that the landlord's consent to sublet or assignment "not be unreasonably withheld." But, does this phrase really help when a landlord is determined to prevent a sublease or assignment? For one thing what is "unreasonable?" Landlords can be very creative when it comes to finding something wrong with a prospective tenant. Second, as a practical matter, even if a landlord is clearly acting unreasonably, few prospective subtenants or assignees will occupy a space or buy a lease without the written approval of the landlord for they cannot take the risk that the landlord will prevail in an eviction action. While the tenant may have a lawsuit against the landlord for unreasonably withholding consent, the prospective subtenant or assignee is probably long gone by the time of the court's decision.

Recapture Clauses
Some landlords are very direct about their intentions, inserting lease clauses such as the following: "In the event that the tenant sublets the leased premises or assigns the lease, any increase over the lease rentals and/or purchase price for the lease (over the cost of tenant improvements) goes to the landlord." Many tenants will not argue with this clause because few enter a lease as real estate players; most are just seeking space to use for their own operations. Accordingly, they don't analyze the profit potential of the lease and are content with a sublet/assignment clause which will allow them to cover their rental obligations in the event they desire to move.

Slices of the Pie

A good real estate player should be aware of the many different interests in a real estate deal on which money can be made. For example, you may be aware of a piece of land which can be leased for 50 years or so. You may lease this land and then obtain financing to construct a building thereon. You may then turn around and master lease the entire building to another real estate player who feels that he can make money subdividing the building into 5,000 square foot areas and subdividing these units. Some other player may sublease one of the 5,000 square foot areas and subsequently sub-sublease it to very small users and make money doing this.

The point is that each of the players makes money by identifying a piece of the pie, gaining control over it, and then leasing or subleasing it at a profit. The good player should always be aware of the many types of potential profit in every real estate deal.[48]

Notes to Chapter 4

1.   Basically, a residential, multifamily property which needs cosmetic renovation and better management, the costs of which will be small when compared to the potential increase in the rent roll.

2.   (Simon & Schuster, 1969). This book has since been updated to *How I Turned $1,000 into Five Million in My Spare Time* (New York: Simon & Schuster, 1980). For another excellent book on revitalizing apartment properties, see Craig Hall's *The Real Estate Turnaround* (Englewood Cliffs, N.J.: Prentice-Hall, 1978).

3.   The passage of money can be important, for a contract is not enforceable unless there is "consideration"—that is, each party gives something of value to the other. Generally, however, money is not required as a promise to purchase (matching the seller's promise to sell), which is sufficient.

4.   I thought that the suggestion of *scrap paper* would make the request seem less preconceived.

5.   Had I more adequately prepared for our luncheon I would have asked around about this individual and learned that his word wasn't exactly his bond.

6.   His lawyer's argument was that it did not sufficiently describe the seller financing which was part of the deal. His lawyer also alleged that the "contract" was unenforceable beacuse I was a lawyer and his client wasn't and that therefore I knew what I was doing and his client did not. The fact of the matter was that the seller was much more knowledgeable than I was at that time in my life (don't assume that three years of law school necessarily prepares one for real-life situations), but the argument was a good one. I never again, by the way, have attempted to put a deal in writing—no matter how simple—without the other party's lawyer being involved.

7.   Time was arguably on my side. If I prevailed in court, albeit three years later, the property would presumably be worth considerably more than my "contract" price.

8.   The courts can also be quite unpredictable. Despite my righteous indignation, I may well have lost the case.

9.   A commonly used term meaning to sell (assign) the contract (the right to buy at a stipulated price) to another party.

10. Known as a liquidated or stipulated damages clause, that is, the parties stipulate what the seller's damages will be in the event of the buyer's default. A more aggressive approach for Buyer would be to attempt to get a clause which states that in the event of Buyer's default Seller's sole and exclusive remedy is to retain so much of Buyer's downpayment as represents Seller's *actual damages* resulting from Buyer's default. This clause requires Seller to establish what his actual damages were, with a cap in the amount of the downpayment. This clause would be particularly important to Buyer in our example because he is buying at a price below market such that it is hard to see how Seller would be damaged by Buyer's default.

11. Buyer should probably also request a provision in the contract permitting him entry into the property—with reasonable notice. He wants this clause so that he can bring

prospective purchasers of his contract through the house. He may have to be creative, however, as to his response if the seller asks why he wants this clause for, a seller who deduces that his buyer will attempt to flip their contract may well realize that he is underselling his property.

12. Buyer must be careful that his attorney not let Seller's attorney know Buyer's game plan: To attempt to flip the contract. This would tell Seller that perhaps his selling price is low. Also, Seller may be thinking that Buyer is a definite buyer and may not appreciate the fact that Buyer may intentionally default. A seller signing a noncontingent contract assumes he has a deal and may both emotionally and physically prepare to move, including going to contract on a new house. The prospect of getting the buyer's downpayment in the event of the buyer's default may not be enough of an inducement to enter a contract if the seller believes the deal will not close.

13. Needless to say, Buyer's option would be even better if he had convinced Seller to agree to a downpayment of less than 10%.

14. Buyer could also buy and resell, but he may not have the financial ability to close. And, selling the contract is much less expensive in that he doesn't incur closing costs upon purchase and resale of the house.

15. Even when the mortgage terms may be available, a buyer who really doesn't exert an all-out effort to get the mortgage can use the contingency in the event he wants to back out of the deal. To counter this, a good seller's attorney should put a clause in the mortgage contingency requiring the buyer to use his "best efforts" to obtain the stipulated mortgage.

16. A knowledgeable seller's attorney should be able to identify these situations for his client, but the fact remains, in my opinion, that only a minority of practicing attorneys are able to match wits with and understand the creativity of a non-lawyer real estate player.

17. His only cost being the expenses of the zoning application.

18. A knowledgeable seller's attorney shouldn't allow this: if the contingency is that the buyer be able to obtain approval for a 1,000 square foot addition, the contract should provide that the buyer *must* apply for a 1,000 square foot addition.

19. Remember that the party whose obligation is subject to a contingency can always waive that contingency and proceed with the deal whether the contingent event occurs or not.

20. This suggestion—to analyze the deal differently than everyone else is doing—is, in my opinion, a critical element of successful entrepreneurship.

21. We also had the right to extend the option period for an additional 60 days upon payment of an additional $25,000. Whenever negotiating an option, always try to get the right to an extension; you don't have to take it, yet you may well need more time than you think.

22. We were still fairly new to real estate game playing and did not yet have a banking relationship.

23. By the way, both the first ($1,100,000) and second ($300,000) mortgages were nonrecourse so that we bought the property without any of our own cash or credit—which was fortunate as we had neither.

24. The owner of the right of first refusal will still have grounds for a legal action against the original owner of the real estate, but this claim may not compensate him for losing the property.

25. The other real estate player wanted the right to step in and take the $1,500,000 deal. It didn't really matter whether the right of first refusal was transferable because the game player could simply have reached an agreement with the

restaurant owner whereby the restaurant owner would exercise his right of first refusal, enter a contract to buy the real
estate for $1,500,000, and then simply assign his contract to
the game player.

26. An offer we were considering matching both because we
felt $1,500,000 (really $1,600,000 with the additional $100,000)
was a good price and because we were now "into the
deal"—emotionally excited about buying and putting our
renovation and marketing ideas to work.

27. Another suggestion: when negotiating to buy property
from an individual who also owns adjoining property, always
ask for a right of first refusal on the adjoining real estate.

28. A sophisticated seller will be aware that a right of first
refusal can depress his sales price because it inhibits potential
buyers and thus chills the bidding for his real estate.

29. On occasion, the first year or so of a retail lease will be a
percentage-rent-only deal (i.e., no minimum rent due)—the
premise being that the new retail tenant needs a year or so to
get his store going.

30. This $500,000 figure came by dividing 5% into the mini-
mum rent of $25,000. While the "break point" is an item to be
negotiated, most of the time it represents the minimum rent
divided by the percentage (this is sometimes termed the
"natural break"). The reason is that retail tenants like to think
of their rent obligation as some established percentage of
their gross sales. So, for instance, the tenant in our example
understands that whether it's in the form of minimum rent
or, percentage rent, he is basically paying rent equal to 5% of
his gross sales—with, however, a minimum guarantee to the
landlord of $25,000.

31. A "gross" rent usually means the tenant makes only that
payment to the landlord (all charges are included within the
rent) which is of course higher-than-market rent (exclusive of
any charges) to compensate the landlord for the additional

items which he pays. A "net," "net net" or "net net net" rental means the tenant makes additional payments to the landlord for, as the case may be, utilities, insurance, real estate taxes, maintenance, operating costs (trash removal, security, snow plowing, landscape care, management, etc.) and any other items the parties agree to. The difference between "net" and "net net" and "net net net" is what additional payments the tenant makes. For example, a "triple net" ("net net net," or "nnn") lease generally means that in addition to its rent, the tenant pays all its own utilities as well as real estate taxes, insurance premiums, and operating and maintenance costs attributable to the real estate of which the leased premises is a part or, a pro rata share thereof if the leased premises is only a portion of the building(s) on improved real estate.

32. The "fee interest" is the legal term for the highest ownership position in a piece of real estate.

33. Some landlords, in their eagerness to lease space, ignore the creditworthiness of the tenant.

34. Sometimes, a landlord will agree to release the tenant if the assignee substitutes its credit for that of the tenant (which credit is presumably as good or better than the tenant's credit).

35. The tenant had bought low and was now selling high! And remember, the original tenant *paid nothing* for the lease—all he did was sign his name. There was, of course, risk in this act in that the tenant obligated himself to 30 years of rental payments. In any event, the $2,500,000 was pure profit for the tenant, on an investment of zero.

36. I am simplifying the example by not calculating the increase in net income due to an increase in market rents. With the use of a computer, one could make certain assumptions about future market values and fairly easily factor these numbers into the analysis.

37. The time remaining on the lease by the time we got the space back and sublet it.

38. See, for example, *Financial Compound Interest and Annuity Tables* (Boston: Financial Publishing Company, 1979).

39. Roughly, any lease of a block of space which is then sublet to various other tenants. In the previous example, the 30,000 square foot lease was a "master lease."

40. There are several reasons why this type of space may be very popular with some people: the need for short-term space; the need for only 100 to 200 square feet (which is generally difficult to find elsewhere); the ease of moving right in (without the need for furniture, phone lines etc.); the attaining of services (e.g. phone answering) which might not otherwise be economical for the small user.

41. Although my company is not in this business, I believe that my estimates, albeit rough are fairly accurate.

42. For simplicity, assume that this rent is gross and that there are no increases in rent during the 20-year lease term.

43. Some of the cost of partitioning and finishing is probably borne by the landlord as this work is usually part of the landlord's "work letter." A work letter is an attachment to the lease which describes how the space will be delivered from the landlord to the tenant.

44. For simplicity I am assuming a self-liquidating, 20-year, $1,000,000 loan at a fixed rate of 12%.

45. "Core area" is the term used to describe that portion of a floor which contains for example, the elevators and stairways and as such is gross but not useable square footage.

46. $750/month is $9,000/year, which when divided by 200 square feet is $45/square foot.

47. Needless to say, there is quite an element of risk. If the "office suite" company's market analysis is wrong (say, the offices can only rent for $500/month or, its vacancy is higher than projected), the above numbers can change dramatically.

48. There are some great stories about successful real estate deals (such as the Empire State Building story) with many different interests in just one deal—the fee (land) owner, the owner of the land lease (who improves the land with a building), the owner of the master lease of a portion of the building, the owner of a sublease of a portion of the building, etc.

5

Tax Benefits:
A Big Added Plus

The New Tax Law

On October 22, 1986, President Reagan signed into law
H.R. 3838, the Tax Reform Bill of 1986, a sweeping change of
the Internal Revenue Code. In many respects, the taxation of
real estate has been altered. This chapter addresses those
changes (as best they can be understood today and with full
awareness that some of the specifics will have to be inter-
preted and tested over time), interweaving a discussion of the
new law with a general outline of taxes and real estate.

As a preliminary matter, I want to note my viewpoint on
taxes and the real estate game. It is my opinion that the real
estate player should not undertake a deal which presents *only*
a tax play, for, in my view, pursuing an investment which is
set up for tax reasons is putting the cart before the horse. Let
the tax benefits of real estate ownership be the icing on the
cake, and keep in mind that, for the real estate player, the
main ingredients of the undertaking should be pure and
simple economics—cash flow, appreciation and equity build-
up.

117

Profit and Loss

The federal income tax that one owes is calculated on the amount of one's "taxable income," that is, "gross income" minus deductions.[1] Thus, deductions are a good thing to have for tax purposes.

Your Own Home

Some real estate deductions represent actual out-of-pocket (compare depreciation, discussed below) expenditures. As an example, two deductions which you may take if you own a home are interest payments on your mortgage, and real estate taxes. These deductions, which represent the amount you actually spend for interest and real estate taxes, are valuable[2] in that the U.S. government is reimbursing you, in part, for these expenditures.

For example, let's assume that in 1986 you paid your mortgage lender $20,000 in interest and your town $4,000 in real estate taxes. Let's also assume that you earned $60,000 in 1986 and that you had no other deductions or exemptions. Due to the interest and tax deductions, your taxable income is reduced from $60,000 to $36,000.

Now, under the new two-tiered Tax Code,[3] taxable income[4] up to $29,750 is taxed at 15% and taxable income above this amount is taxed at a rate of 28%.[5] So, in our example, the $24,000 worth of deductions from home ownership saves our taxpayer $6,720.

$60,000 Taxable Income		*$36,000 Taxable Income*	
	Tax		**Tax**
$29,750 × .15 =	$4,462.50	$29,750 × .15 =	$4,462.50
$30,250 × .28 =	$8,470.00	$ 6,250 × .28 =	$1,750.00
$60,000	$12,932.50	$36,000	$6,212.50

SAVINGS = $12,932.50 − $6,212.50 = $6,720.00

As you can see, the difference is considerable. The new Code has made one major change in the deduction of mortgage interest payments on one's home; for the first time there is a limit[6] on the total amount of mortgage interest deductible. The new law provides that a homeowner may only deduct interest due on a mortgage loan or loans the total of which do not exceed the original cost of the home plus improvements.[7]

Second or Vacation Homes

So long as another residence is used by the taxpayer as a dwelling for part of the year (generally, in excess of 14 days or 10 percent of the number of days of rental use, whichever is greater), it can qualify as a second home and the interest on loans against it—limited, however, as with principal residences—is deductible.

Investment Properties

Gains and Out of Pocket Losses

In order to understand the tax treatment of investment property, you should set out the property's annual revenues and out-of-pocket expenses. One example follows:

Income
  Rent: $50,000

Expenses
  Taxes   ($ 3,500)
  Insurance   (2,000)
  Maintenance/Repair   (2,000)
  Interest[8]   (35,000)
  Miscellaneous   (1,500)

                                                     (44,500)

TOTAL INCOME (LOSS): $ 5,500

In this example (ignoring depreciation or any other passive loss for the moment), the $5,500 income from the property is added to the property owner's taxable income on which he will pay taxes of 15%, 28% or 33%.

Now, what happens if there is a loss? Say, for example, the numbers on the property look like this:

Income
Rent		$50,000

Expenses
Taxes	($ 4,500)	
Insurance	(3,000)	
Maintenance/repair	(3,500)	
Interest	(45,000)	
Miscellaneous	(2,500)	
		($58,500)

TOTAL INCOME (LOSS):	($ 8,500)

It is in this situation that the new tax law has made major changes. In the past, the $8,500 loss would be deductible, reducing one's taxable income by this amount. Such is no longer the law.[9]

Now, with one exception (below), this $8,500 is categorized: Loss from rental property is termed *passive* loss which can only offset "passive" income. Non-"passive" income such as salary and "portfolio" income (money earned, for example, from stocks, bonds, savings accounts, financial instruments) can no longer be sheltered (offset) by losses from rental property. This does not mean that the $8,500 loss has no value to the taxpayer; the loss can offset passive income,[10] such as cash flow (our first example) from other properties. In addition, the $8,500 loss can be carried forward into future years and used against any cash flow or gain on sale generated from the property now showing a loss.

As mentioned, there is one exception to the rule that "passive" loss may only offset "passive" income. In the event that: (a) the taxpayer is deemed an "active participant"[11] in his rental property; and (b) has an adjusted gross income of less than $100,000,[12] then he can use up to $25,000 of rental property loss to offset non-passive income.

Depreciation
So far we have talked only about out-of-pocket expenses (interest, taxes, maintenance, etc.) relative to ownership of a

rental property. But there is a very significant "paper" expense (no one actually reaches into his pocket to pay for this) which the Internal Revenue Code attributes to real estate.[13] This "expense" is known as depreciation, the concept being that the portion[14] of the cost of one's real estate allocable to the physical improvements thereon (land is not depreciable) deteriorates every year. The annual "cost" of this deterioration is the yearly depreciation "expense."

Any building "put in service" prior to January 1, 1987, could take advantage of the old, more favorable depreciation rules, specifically that the improvements were deemed to have a "useful life" of 19 years[15] and, therefore, that each year the building had a taxable expense of 1/19 of its original cost. The new depreciation rules mandate a useful life of 27.5 years for residential property[16] and 31.5 years for non-residential property. Thus, the annual depreciation expense has dropped from about 5.3% (1/19) to 3.6% (1/27.5) for residential property and 3.1% (1/31.5) for non-residential property.

Let's see how depreciation affects our income and expense statement. In our first example, let's assume the subject property is non-residential and that it has a cost[17] of $400,000 of which 80% or $320,000 is allocable to improvements.[18] So, our annual depreciation expense would be $320,000 divided by 31.5 or $10,159, and our income and expense statement will look like this:

Income
Rent $ 50,000

Expenses
  Taxes   ($ 3,500)
  Insurance   (2,000)
  Maintenance/Repair   (2,500)
  Interest   (35,000)
  Miscellaneous   (1,500)
  Depreciation   (10,159)

                                                        (54,659)

TOTAL INCOME (LOSS)   ($ 4,659)

So, the effect of the depreciation was to turn an *actual* dollars and cents profit of $5,500 into a *taxable* loss of $4,659. Accordingly, the property owner not only pays no tax on his $5,500 profit but also has a $4,659 loss to use against passive income from other rental properties or future income from this property (by way of cash flow or gain on sale). Here you can see the value of the depreciation "expense" even with the new, elongated "useful life."

On the sale of real estate, depreciation is theoretically recaptured. The logic here is that if, in fact, there was no actual loss due to depreciation, the taxpayer should repay the amount by which he depreciated the building. The system works this way: The purchase price of real estate plus closing costs and improvements minus depreciation is the "adjusted basis" of the property. On sale, the adjusted basis is subtracted from the net sales price (gross sales price minus selling costs) in order to determine the gain on sale. In the above example, we had a basis of $400,000 and $10,159 of annual depreciation expense. Let's assume that this property was held for three years and then sold. The adjusted basis would thus be $400,000 − $30,477[19] = $369,523. So if, let's say, the net sales price is $500,000, the gain on sale is $130,477.

In addition to depreciating real property (again, improvements, not land), a taxpayer can depreciate personal property which he uses as part of the real estate but which is not attached to the real estate. Since the life expectancy of personalty is less than 31 years, it can generate an annual expense greater than 1/31 of its value. Accordingly, some real estate players will lease their buildings with moveable interior partitions (rather than fixed walls) or area rugs (rather than carpeting affixed to the floor) and depreciate these items of personalty over five to ten years rather than 31 years. The result is greater annual "expenses" (remember, as to depreciation, no one actually reaches in their pocket).

Gain on Sale

Up until the new law, owners of real estate were accorded a very favorable tax preference in that only 40% of (long-term) capital gains were subject to taxation. The new law deletes this preference. Now, gain on sale of real property is taxed at the same rates as all other income—15%, 28% or 33%.[20]

Identifying the Gain

As we discussed above, the gain on sale is the difference between the net sales price and the taxpayer's "basis" (more accurately, "adjusted basis") on sale. Remember that the adjusted basis is the original basis of the property—purchase price plus closing costs[21]—plus improvements and minus depreciation.

It is important to see that actual gain on sale and taxable gain on sale are two different things. Actual gain is not increased by the amount of depreciation; therefore, a taxpayer who has taken a great deal of depreciation against a building must be ready to pay taxes on a taxable gain which may be much larger than his actual gain. For example, suppose you have owned an office building for five years. Let's say that you bought it for $200,000 and it is now worth $300,000 (or $270,000 net of closing costs on sale). Let's say that over the five years you depreciated the building by $25,000. Thus, your adjusted basis is now $175,000. On sale you have a taxable gain of $95,000 but an actual gain of only $70,000 and taxes due on sale (assume 28% bracket) of almost $27,000, which uses up almost one-half of your actual gain.

This illustration is not meant to highlight a negative point; we have already seen the great advantages of depreciation. The point here is to suggest that before a sale you review the tax status of your property and be aware of your adjusted basis and potential *taxable* gain on sales. Don't be caught unaware, as are some people, who during their ownership either refinance or put additional financing against their property, taking out all or a good portion of their actual (cash) gain, and learn at closing that their actual gain on sale is not enough to cover the taxes due. As an example, let's say you bought the above office building with $25,000 cash and a $175,000 mortgage and that three years after purchase you took a second mortgage of $75,000 (assume both mortgages are interest only). Now you sell for $300,000 and net

$270,000, but you must use $250,000 to pay off your mortgages. The result is that you have $20,000 in actual dollars left to meet a tax liability (see above) of approximately $27,000.

Timing the Gain

A good real estate player will consider the timing of the sale of his real estate in order to minimize the tax consequences thereof. For example, let's assume that you want to sell a piece of property and you know that your taxable gain on sale will be approximately $100,000 and that (if you are in the 28% bracket) your tax liability will be $28,000. When should you sell? Well, if you close in December 1987, you must include the income in your 1987 return and pay the taxes in April 1988. On the other hand, if you close in January 1988, you include the income within your 1988 return and pay the taxes in April 1989. Thus, closing on or after January 1, 1987, means that you have an additional 12 months to use the money due the government. A good real estate player can use this additional 12 months to turn the $28,000 into $56,000 or more.

Up until the new Act, some real estate players would spread out the taxation of gain on sale by use of the "installment method." The benefits of the use of this accounting procedure have been dramatically curtailed under the new law.[22]

Tax Credits

A credit is more valuable than a deduction. Whereas a deduction offsets income, a credit offsets taxes due. Thus a credit is about three times as valuable as a deduction. For example, if you are in the 28% bracket, each dollar of deduction is worth $.28 to you because it offsets $1.00 of income, which $1.00 would have cost you $.28 in taxes. In contrast, each dollar of credit is worth $1.00 of tax savings because a credit offsets bottom-line taxes due. Thus for the taxpayer in the 28% bracket, a tax credit is worth more than three times as much as a deduction.

There are now three sections in the Internal Revenue Code pursuant to which a player may attain tax credits[23]:

Historical Renovation

Upon the renovation of a structure which is a "certified historic structure" and upon completing renovations which are "certified rehabilitation expenditures," the owner receives a one-time credit equal to 20% of the costs of renovation. Needless to say, this credit is very valuable and if not needed by the real estate player/renovator, can be used to attract partners/investors.[24]

Although opinions differ, some real estate players will not undertake these historical renovations because of the bureaucracy and time delays in "qualifying" the expenditures. Delay can, of course, be very costly because most real estate players aggressively finance their projects and thus have a tremendous incentive to renovate and rent quickly.

1935 or Older Buildings[25]

The second section deals with the renovation of buildings placed in service in 1935 or before. Here, a tax credit of 10% of the costs of renovation can be obtained provided that the owner keeps in place 75% of the building's existing external walls as well as 75% of the internal structural framework.

Low-income Housing Credit

Starting in 1987, there is a new tax credit available with respect to low-income housing.[26] This new section provides three opportunities by which one can obtain a tax credit each year for ten years:

- 9% (per year) of expenditures incurred for new construction and rehabilitation of low-income housing units.
- 4% (per year) of expenditures incurred for new construction and rehabilitation of low-income housing units

financed with tax-exempt bonds or other federal subsidies.
- 4% (per year) of the cost of acquisition of low-income housing units in an existing project.

Money That Is Not "Income"

Every year many real estate players put a lot of money in their pockets that is not taxable at all because it is not considered "income" for purposes of the Internal Revenue Code. Money that a taxpayer borrows is not considered income. Therefore, mortgage debt[27] is not normally considered income. Because real estate is a highly financeable asset, there are many opportunities for the real estate player to obtain tax-free dollars.[28]

Many real estate players finance out considerable sums of money from their properties (some do it annually), paying no taxes on the proceeds. The negative of this practice is, of course, that the cash flow from the property must be able to carry the increased debt service which goes with the increased debt.

Tax-free Exchanges

There is no tax consequence from the transfer of real estate for other real estate of like kind.[29] However, to the extent real estate is traded for other real estate *and* money, there is a recognizable gain to the extent of the amount of money. This section of the code is, in reality, only a deferral of taxes, for the basis of the new property is deemed to be the basis of the old property (as of the date of the trade) so that sooner or later (when the new property is sold) the owner must recognize a taxable gain based on the original property's basis.

My experience has been that exchanging is quite cumbersome and used by very few real estate players. Nevertheless, in terms of overall tax planning, it is a way to defer taxes due on the "sale" of real property.

Partnerships and Disproportionate Allocation

As mentioned above, one way for a real estate player to attract capital is to form a partnership. And one tool available for doing this is his ability to disproportionately allocate the potential tax loss from the property.

The IRS takes the position that one (or more) partner(s) may take a larger share of the tax loss (than he takes of the other ownership interests, e.g., cash flow, profit on sale) if there is substantial "economic effect" to this allocation. Economic effect generally means that there must be some financial logic as to why one owner should get substantially more tax loss than another and this logic must carry through to the operation and liquidation phases of the venture. Usually, the fact that one partner puts up 90% of the capital needed to purchase the real estate is considered sufficient justification for allocating to that person 90% of the tax loss (and so long as that person also recognizes *taxable* gain on sale which corresponds to those losses). Needless to say, when setting up a partnership with a disproportionate allocation of tax loss, it is a good idea to seek the assistance of a knowledgeable accountant.

Operating in the partnership form, a general partner can, at times, obtain "tax-free" money. In a partnership each partner has a "capital account" which tracks his tax status in the property, and through capital accounting a player can obtain "tax-free" money, debiting his account by the amount of investment capital account which he pockets, and crediting the investor's account. On sale, both accounts must be brought to zero before profits are divided. But, until sale, the player has received money which is tax-"free"[30]—it's not considered income as there is a corresponding debit against the player's partnership capital account.

At-risk Rules and Financing

For the last several years real estate was one of the few investment vehicles available in which an investor's losses could exceed the amount he had at risk (for example, as a limited partner or with non-recourse financing). The Tax Reform Act changed this: With the exception of "qualified non-recourse financing"[31] one's taxable total losses from the ownership of real estate may not exceed one's total risk. This new rule further batters the "tax shelter" syndication business—already badly bruised by the new law's restrictions on the use of passive loss.

Notes to Chapter 5

1.   "Taxable income" is actually "gross income" minus adjustments which yields "adjusted gross income" minus itemized deductions and exemptions.

2.   Keep in mind that most of what you spend is not deductible: food, clothing, utilities, travel. Nor are rent payments for housing deductible.

3.   There is a one-year phase-in of the new tax rates; what follows are the rates for the calendar year beginning January 1, 1988.

4.   For married couples filing joint returns.

5.   There is also a 5% surcharge which is applied to taxable income between $71,900 and $171,090 (married couple with no children filing joint return), although an individual taxpayer's total tax cannot exceed 28% of his taxable income (the 5% surcharge and the 15% rate up to $29,750 average out at 28%).

6.   The intent of this limitation is to prevent homeowners from borrowing against their house to finance consumer purchases (cars, boats, etc.), the interest on borrowing for which is no longer deductible.

7.   As always, there is an exception: The interest on borrowing against one's house for education or medical purposes is deductible without limitation.

8.   Debt repayment (principal) is not considered an operating expense of the property.

9.   There is, however, a four-year phase-out of the use of rental property (investment) loss to offset other (non-passive) income. In 1987 rental property loss is 65% deductible; in 1988, 40%; in 1989, 20%; in 1990, 10%; thereafter none of the loss is deductible.

10. It is not clear what income might be "passive" other than rental property cash flow or gain on sale.

11. The key to being an "active participant" seems to be involvement in the decision-making regarding the property. Needless to say, with the possible exception of limited partners in limited partnerships which own property, there will be very few non-involved real-estate partners in the United States next year (it's hard to see how any non-partner/non-investor owner of real estate can be anything but an "active participant").

12. If the taxpayer has an adjusted gross income of more than $100,000 but less than $150,000, he can still use a portion of the maximum $25,000 loss; if his adjusted gross income is in excess of $150,000, the exception doesn't apply.

13. As well as other tangible assets. What's important to see about depreciation and real estate is that while most depreciable (tangible) assets do *in fact* lose value (wear and tear; obsolescence) over time, real estate continues to appreciate, rendering the depreciation "loss" a fiction.

14. The taxpayer's incentive is therefore to allocate as much as possible of his property's cost to improvements, not land. This allocation can be a matter of dispute, and in such instances an appraisal may be helpful to the taxpayer.

15. The old law also permitted "accelerated" methods of depreciation (faster in the initial years of ownership than the 19-year straight-line method). These methods are no longer permitted for property "put in service" after January 1, 1987.

16. Remember, this must be *investment* property.

17. The terminology of the Internal Revenue Code is "basis"; at this juncture we can assume that "basis" is roughly synonymous with cost.

18. Although we haven't shown it in our example, closing costs attributable to the acquisition of property are also depreciable (see below).

19. $10,159 \times 3 = $30,477.

20. Remember, these are marginal rates (only on income above a certain level). The new Act specifically provides that total tax as a percentage of total adjusted gross income cannot exceed 28%. In 1987, a transition year when effective rates can reach 38.5% (as some deductions are phased out before new lower tax rates are phased in), the law provides that, as to capital gains recognized in 1987, the maximum effective rate is 28%.

21. With respect to an investment property, all closing costs (including origination fee/"points") are added to the basis. As part of the basis, the closing costs (excluding points) can be depreciated over the same period as is the building. The portion of closing costs which is depreciable is that same percentage which the real estate improvements bear to the total purchase price. (Thus, if 80% of the purchase price is allocated to the improvements, then 80% of the closing costs are depreciable.) With respect to points, they are amortized (expensed annually in an amount equal to 100% of their cost divided by the years of the loan) over the life of the loan.

22. Suffice it to say for the purposes of this chapter that the new installment method is so unwieldy as to make it unlikely that a real estate player will want to structure a sale around it.

23. These new provisions apply to property "placed in service" after December 31, 1986. It should also be noted that the credit phases out for upper-income taxpayers: The phase-

out begins when a taxpayer has an adjusted gross income of $200,000 and is fully eliminated when adjusted gross income reaches $250,000.

24. For example, let's say that qualified renovation expenditures are $250,000, such that there is a credit of $50,000. If the real estate player does not need this credit, he can use it to raise partnership capital. Suppose, for example, that he offers 90% ($45,000) of the credit to a prospective investor in return for a $200,000 investment in the partnership. Without even considering what other aspects of ownership are offered, we see that the investor receives more than 20% of his investment back in year one of the partnership, a very attractive lure for partnership capital, especially when the deal can be structured such that the investment is made at the end of the year in which the tax credit is received.

25. As to the renovation of historic structures and 50-year-old property, the "old-law" restrictions on resale still appear to apply: Even though the full amount of the credit may be taken in the year that the property is put into service, five years must pass before the credit is irrevocably earned. The credit is essentially "earned" 20% per year for five years.

26. To qualify as "low-income" housing, either: a) at least 20% of the units in the project must be occupied by individuals having incomes 50% or less than the area median income, or b) at least 40% of the units in the project must be occupied by individuals having incomes 60% or less than area median income.

27. This rule is applied to even non-recourse debt—debt which is secured only by the real estate and thus money which one has no personal obligation to repay.

28. Some will argue that the correct terminology is "tax-deferred" dollars for, sooner or later, one must pay taxes on the equity which was financed out. For example, suppose Jones owns a building with a market value of $1,000,000, a mortgage of $500,000 and an adjusted basis of $300,000. He

has $500,000 equity, and he decides to draw some of it out by taking a $300,000 second mortgage. This is not a taxable event as the $300,000 is a debt and thus is not income. Those who argue "tax-deferred" say that sooner or later Jones must sell (even if he defaults, his "gain" is any debt forgiven over his adjusted basis), and when he does, his $300,000 second mortgage will be taxed. In our example, if Jones sells soon after taking the second mortgage, his taxable gain is $700,000 even though his actual gain is only $200,000. In other words, on sale Jones "pays the piper" because he is then taxed on the tax-free debt (the $300,000) which he received at some prior time. Still, Jones controls the timing of the sale and thus the circumstances under which he pays for the tax-free (deferred) money.

29. Section 1031(a) of the Internal Revenue Code: "No gain or loss shall be recognized if property held for productive use in trade or business or for investment . . . is exchanged solely for property of a like kind to be held either for productive use in trade or business or for investment."

30. Remember the "tax-deferred" argument as it applies to "tax-free" debt, for it applies here as well.

31. "Qualified non-recourse financing": generally, nonrecourse debt as advanced by a third party (not the seller) lender.

6

Location and Zoning

Location

Probably you've heard the statement:

"The three most important things in real estate are location, location and location."

I don't believe that this rule is an absolute for the good real estate player although location is certainly an important element of most game plans.

The point about location is that it's better to buy in the middle of Manhattan than in the middle of the Bronx. But everybody knows that and if everybody could buy in the middle of Manhattan, perhaps they would. What's important to us is how the real estate player can use location to his advantage in an attempt to score on a deal.

As an investor, location should be the number one factor in deciding on a property. Pure investors should buy only in good, solid, stable locations which should yield good, solid, predictable returns. And, the investor will, of course, pay well for this stability and predictability. The real estate player, on the other hand, has to create his own value and is generally not interested in paying absolute top dollar for a premier location—then waiting for inflation and appreciation to take over. This difference in approach illustrates an important distinction between the investor and the real estate player: the investor waits for inflation/appreciation to happen; the real estate player attempts to make it happen.

The real estate player may attempt to score on a deal by acquiring property in a marginal location, which area he believes to be on the way up. In this way, the value of his real estate increases not only by the usual forces (inflation, supply-demand, psychology of expectations) but also by the extraordinary demand and buying fervor which eventually flows to an area on the upswing. The result is an increased value in multiples; in other words, by taking a risk on location, the player attempts to realize an increase in value far beyond traditional returns. And, the greater the risk the player is willing to take—that is, the earlier he buys into such an area—the lower the prices and the greater the potential for a score. The key is to buy in an area on the upswing. But how do you identify these areas?

Identifying the Upswing Areas[1]
Talk to municipal officials (e.g., mayor, zoning officer)
Are there big things planned for any part of the city? Many cities and towns today are trying to clean up blighted areas and are spending their own money to do so. They are also offering tax abatements and other incentives to attract private investment into these areas.

Talk to other players
Is the smart money starting to flow into a heretofore unexciting part of the city? Notwithstanding a lot of apparent player excitement, be careful of what I call the "new area hype." Sometimes one or more players will begin buying (or acquiring options) in an area and will then do everything possible to attract other money and development to the area.[2] Soon you may start hearing:

Jones: "I can't believe the money going into the south side!"

Smith: "I just scored on three contracts—flipped them before closing!"

Adams: "Have you heard? They say Donald Trump is starting to buy property on the south side. He's not using his own name, of course."

You may wish to take this "information" with a grain of salt. Some of it may well be true; some of it, however, may be exaggeration or distortion. The point is that while local real estate players may be the first to know things about an area of the city, they may also have an economic interest in generating excitement in and to this area. Listen carefully and then attempt to confirm what you've heard.

Look for physical signs
Do you see signs of private investment? Do you see signs of renewed pride and attention from the current residents? Look for renovation. Look for improved maintenance—even new painting is good. Many times an upward turn is started not by the city or by developers but by a new interest and excitement in an area from its own residents. An influx of young professionals into an area, seeking moderate priced housing, is almost always a good sign as well, for these upwardly mobile individuals bring with them energy, pride and money.

Where are the directions of progress?
Many times good common sense can tell you that an area has to improve sooner or later. Such things as proximity to an interstate highway or a beautiful waterfront should tell you something. Also, is the area in a line with past development—is it just to the east of a succession of improved areas immediately to the west? Needless to say, before you can make a very informed judgment on these points you must familiarize yourself with the city, its surrounding areas and the history of its growth.

Federal and State Enterprise Zones
The U.S. and many state governments have designated certain areas as "enterprise zones" to encourage private in-

vestment in these areas. The enterprise zones offer savings or abatements on state and federal taxes. Are there areas of the city currently so designated? Are there areas under consideration? Is the city actively working to obtain "enterprise" designation for an area?

Check the land records

As described in the next chapter, once you know your way around the city clerk's office, and specifically how to use the land records, you can learn a tremendous amount about any area. Identify the streets within the area you are considering and then use the land records to ascertain the number of sales and the prices. The frequency of sales as well as the prices during the prior year or so should tell you something very important about an area.

The point is to identify those areas of your town, city or state which are about to take off (or have just taken off but still have plenty of room for price increase). By getting in on the ground floor, you put yourself in a position to realize an increase in value many times greater than normal appreciation.

When and How to Buy?

The question of when to buy highlights a situation in the real estate game where there is a direct correlation between risk and reward. The earlier (and more aggressively) you buy into an area's "upswing," the greater your chance for a real score. But the earlier you buy, the greater the risk for, you simply may be wrong. Maybe the signs you identify are misleading. Maybe something unpredictable will occur which will kill or delay the development of the area. If so, you could be stuck with an illiquid or even depreciating position.

Therefore, in betting on location, you must also analyze risk. Consider the downside and your overall position in the event your projection doesn't pan out. Perhaps you will want to limit your investment to $X until you get a better feel for the area. If possible, it may be preferable to acquire an option rather than to make an outright purchase. The point is that the analysis should be in two parts: one, identifying the right area; two, quantifying the risk.

Checking the Property

Before committing to any purchase,[3] you must check the property:

1. If land, is the property "buildable?" Is there rock?[4] Is the land too wet to support a building.[5] Is the water table too high to handle a septic system?

2. If a building, are the structure and systems in good condition? Before signing a contract or waiving a building inspection contingency, you should (at the least) have an inspection made of the roof and foundation, and the HVAC,[6] plumbing, electric, and septic (or sewage) systems. You may think that you have found the perfect property until you discover hidden costs of repair and/or replacement. The building inspection is also a good opportunity to identify projected renovation costs, if that is your game.[7]

3. In considering a purchase, you should, of course, also review the zoning status of the property. And you should consider not just the current use but also your contemplated usage(s). For example, you may find that the existent usage is legally nonconforming[8] and therefore not up to current zoning rules. Your concern in that case should be any provision in the zoning code which requires that a nonconformity be brought "up to code" if there is a change in the physical structure or usage of a property. Therefore, it is critical for you to analyze the zoning situation in terms of your eventual game plan for the property. In addition to zoning, you should review all other applicable municipal regulations[9] to insure against surprises.

Zoning

It is difficult to generalize about zoning because each city has its own particular zoning rules and regulations. This fact means opportunity for the real estate player who becomes knowledgeable in the rules and regulations of a particular zoning code. Armed with more knowledge than other individuals who are selling or buying, the informed player can use this imbalance to create opportunity.

Imbalance of Knowledge

For example, many sellers will offer a piece of land for sale at a price which reflects their understanding of its development potential. But they may not know all the tricks of the zoning game and they may in fact grossly underestimate the potential of their site. In addition, if other potential buyers are not as savvy as you are, they may not be able to accurately evaluate the seller's price. But, if you know that by taking a new approach to the zoning application (currently favored by the local zoning board), you have a good chance to obtain approval for more building area than that anticipated by the seller (and other buyers), you are at a distinct advantage. You may very well score on such a deal by buying at a price reflecting the seller's analysis of buildable square footage[10] (say, 10,000 square feet at $50/square foot, or $500,000) when in fact you can actually obtain zoning approval to build 13,000 square feet (worth $50/square foot x 13,000 = $650,000); score of $150,000). This is an example of the kind of return you can earn on the time you invest in becoming expert in the particular zoning rules and regulations of a given area.

Creating Opportunities

Zoning is also an area of great opportunity for the creative player willing to take a risk on obtaining difficult zoning approvals. Considerable sums of money have been made by players who took a shot at a "long-shot" development difficult zoning approval, rezoning or, variance.[11] And the risk involved in making these attempts can be minimized by acquiring an option or a contract with a zoning contingency.

Zoning Applications and Hearings

In my opinion, there are some general rules in proceeding with a zoning application and hearing.

Anticipate and Prepare

In any controversial application, anticipate and prepare yourself for neighborhood opposition. Even if the neighborhood's objections are obviously founded in self-interest, totally unreasonable, and contrary to the intent and interpretation of the city zoning code, most zoning boards will listen carefully to neighbor complaints. Rarely is the real estate player the favored party before a local zoning board deluged with neighborhood opposition to a project.

In this regard, I recommend that you attempt to meet with and pacify the neighborhood prior to the hearing. If that doesn't work, and even if the criticism at the zoning hearing of your project is very vocal and strident, I suggest that you not attack your critics head on. Remember that the zoning board is made up of individuals who live in a neighborhood somewhere and are thus sensitive to neighborhood interests. Attacking your critics directly may well backfire and antagonize the zoning board. I believe that a recitation of the neighborhood concerns and how you answer or intend to minimize each is a much better approach than public argument.

I experienced the weight of neighborhood criticism within a year of entering the real estate game. Two friends and I wanted to renovate a dilapidated building in a nice residential neighborhood. All of the neighbors except one supported us and that neighbor wanted money ($10,000) for his support. We refused to pay, believing that the zoning board couldn't help but see the merit in our application and at the same time see through this neighbor's objections. On the night of the hearing we made our presentation and one by one the neighbors (seven or eight of them) stood up and successively supported our application. Then the dissenter stood up and made an impassioned speech against changing the neighborhood in which he had lived for 20 years and against the *greed*[12] of developers like us. Although we didn't directly mention the neighbor's request for money,[13] we countered by trying to isolate this individual and showing how unreasonable he was. In sum, our presentation was logical, well researched and well presented—everyone told us so. We lost. I never again underestimated the power of neighborhood opposition.

Keep Your Presentation Short and Simple

Most zoning boards are made up of ordinary members of the community who have no particular zoning expertise. Usually these board members are elected and *unpaid*. The last thing they want is a long-winded, overly detailed presentation. They want to get home. Try not to overwhelm them with your expertise or stamina.

Be Very Courteous

I am always amazed by the presentations of people whose only concern seems to be a display of their public speaking ability. At times, I have seen presenters be aggressive and discourteous to members of the zoning board. These people seem to forget why they are there: to win the *approval* of the zoners. While styles certainly can differ, I recommend a low-key, courteous but firm manner.

Be Prepared

Whatever you do, don't waste anyone's time. Have everything you may need at your fingertips and be prepared to answer any questions. Needless to say, be very familiar with your application and how the zoning rules and regulations apply.

All of the above suggestions are common sensical but often forgotten in the heat of the moment. As a zoning approval can be extremely important to a deal's success or failure, so can the handling of the zoning application/public hearing. Accordingly, do plenty of preparation and handle yourself in a manner solely designed to obtain a favorable decision.

Notes to Chapter 6

1. The hereinafter analysis presumes that you have identified a city/town in which you'd like to play the game. Identifying the right city/town can, however, also be a challenge because not all areas will have (or will have sections within which have) the same potential for an upswing. In selecting a city/town (or, heretofore undeveloped area) in which to concentrate (besides considering proximity and familiarity) you might perform the same type of hereinafter described analysis (as to selecting an area within a city) in asking yourself whether the city/town (or undeveloped area) has considerable upside potential.

2. Their game plan may be to create excitement and demand for a new area in an attempt to make huge profits by reselling when the area becomes "hot" and buying fever pushes up prices dramatically.

3. This doesn't mean that you can't go to contract or otherwise tie up the property. But you must insert a contingency to your obligation to buy that protects you in the event you are not satisfied as to any of the items which need to be checked. For example: "Buyer's obligation hereunder is contingent upon its reasonable satisfaction with a building inspection to be completed within 4 days."

4. Blasting may be possible, but it can be very expensive.

5. Usually you can build on wet land with the use of piles (long telephone pole-like logs which are driven into the ground until they meet enough resistance to support a building); again, however, the issue is one of cost.

6. Common acronym for heating, ventilation and air conditioning systems.

7. Here is an example of tying a property up and using a building inspection contingency to take a free ride (albeit usually very limited in duration) in order to determine whether a renovation makes economic sense.

8.   That it pre-dates the adoption of the applicable zoning rules and regulations.

9.   There may be separate rules and/or commissions on environmental impact, traffic generation, architecture, etc.

10. Many development sites are priced according to the number of square feet which can be built at that site. For example, in the area of the country in which our company operates, the land is sold at $50/square foot of potential (office) building, or $50 "per buildable foot." Thus a piece of land on which can be built 10,000 square feet of office space will sell for $500,000.

11. A variance is a waiver of the zoning rules as they apply in a particular situation. Generally, to obtain a variance, one must illustrate "hardship."

12. Needless to say we could hardly sit still.

13. A decision we rethought and discussed many times. I still believe that mentioning the request (although it bordered on blackmail) raised the risk of muddying the waters and antagonizing the zoners to the point of creating a negativism toward the project.

7

Conveyancing

The transfer of the legal title to real estate is known as conveyancing. It is important to have a basic understanding of this subject in order to play the game well.

Deeds

Information in the Deed

Legal title to real estate is transferred by means of a document known as a deed. The deed names the seller[1] and the buyer, and includes the legal description of the real estate. Sometimes the sales price is also indicated but this information is not required.

A good real estate player/buyer will be sensitive to the nature of the information contained in the deed into him since, immediately after closing, the deed is recorded (put in the public records) and thus becomes public knowledge. For this reason, a player who is trying to assemble several parcels in an area may take title in different/or fictitious names[2] so as to hide from the world the fact that one buyer is acquiring the parcels.[3] Similarly, a buyer who wants to acquire more property within a given area, may not disclose the sales price in deeds into him if, for example, he doesn't want potential sellers (of property in which he's interested) to know how much he paid for property nearby.[4] In this regard, all states permit the deed to make reference only to the fact of consideration—an acknowledgment that there was money conveyed—by a reference such as "for One Dollar ($1.00) and other valuable consideration".[5]

The legal description of the property should be checked against a title search or title insurance binder by an attorney, escrow company, or title company handling the transfer. The description can be "metes and bounds"[6] or, refer to a recorded map.[7] In addition to reviewing this description, you may also want to get a survey[8] (essentially a drawing of the perimeters of the land and the location of the improvements thereon) to be sure that what you *think* you are to receive[9] is what *in fact* you will receive.[10]

Each state has its own laws concerning the formalities required for the proper execution of a deed. The variations relate to the number of witnesses who must sign the deed and whether notarization is required.

Types of Deeds

There are three or four different types of deeds commonly used in the United States. Perhaps you have heard of "warranty deeds," "quit-claim deeds," or "bargain and sale deeds." The differences in the deeds pertain to the liability of the grantor[11] for title problems which are discovered after the closing.

If, for example, the grantor gives a warranty deed, he "warrants," or stands behind, the title to the real estate as described in the deed. If, after the closing, the grantee's ownership (title) is challenged or if an encumbrance is discovered which was not mentioned in the deed, then the grantor can be sued for the grantee's damages. On the other hand, with a quit-claim deed all the grantor says is: "I'm giving you whatever I've got but I'm making *no* representations as to what it is." Therefore, the grantee of the quit-claim deed can never sue the grantor in the event of any later discovered title problems. Every player should have a general knowledge of the types of deeds used in his state although, in the event of a title problem, it is likely that the first place the player will turn is to his title insurance—not to the grantor.[12]

Rights and Encumbrances

A real estate title can be "together with" certain rights and/or "subject to" certain encumbrances. These phrases describe benefits that come with ownership, for example, Jones' right to passage over Smith's land, or burdens on the ownership, for example, Smith's obligation to allow Jones' passage. There are a tremendous variety of rights and encumbrances which can attach to a piece of real estate: easements, restrictive covenants, licenses, rights-of-way, air and water rights, etc., etc. The player's objective is to research the title[13] and discover any rights or encumbrances in advance so as not to be surprised; you may just find an encumbrance which your seller "forgot" to mention or, that a right[14] which you were told went with the property "in perpetuity" had, in point of fact, expired. The prudent course, in my opinion, is to review a title search or preliminary title insurance binder before committing to purchase.[15]

Recordation

The system for preserving real estate documentation, used throughout the United States, is known as recordation. Recordation also means disclosure to the world such that the chronology of recording prioritizes the claims to a piece of real estate. For this reason, the first deed recorded (which conveys ownership to a piece of real estate) will have priority over any later recorded deed *even if* representing a sale which occurred *after* a perfectly legitimate *prior* sale (unless Buyer #2 knew about the sale to Buyer #1).[16] Every document recorded is copied and then bound into books, referenced by volume and page. Therefore, every document ever recorded is available for your inspection once you learn its volume and page.

Grantor-Grantee Indices

The place of recordation is the town, city or county clerk's office. Here you will find copies of every document ever recorded. And, you will find huge volumes known as the grantor and grantee indices, essentially the tables of contents of everything in the clerk's office.

Every document has a grantor and a grantee. In a deed, the seller is the grantor, the buyer the grantee. In a mortgage deed, the mortgagor (borrower) is the grantor and the mortgagee (lender) the grantee. In an involuntary "conveyance," such as an attachment,[17] *lis pendens,*[18] or judgment lien, the property owner is the grantor and the holder of the lien[19] is the grantee. The logic is to treat any document which affects property rights, whether voluntary or not, as a "grant" from the owner, thus making the owner the grantor.

Using the Clerk's Office

A good real estate player should learn his way around the local clerk's office and specifically, how to use the grantor and grantee indices. As discussed, the grantor index will reveal every document which a property owner "grants" (voluntarily or involuntarily) against his real estate. Therefore, suppose you are interested in a piece of real estate and you want to know more about it. First, you trace the deed into the current owner.[20] From the deed you know how long the current owner has owned the property and what he bought it for. You will also see the legal description of the property as well as any rights or encumbrances. Then, checking forward in the grantor index from the date that the owner acquired title, you will see what "grants" the owner put against his property. You will learn about his mortgages—the dates and amounts.[21] You will learn about any involuntary liens against his property. You may also pick up information on leases[22] or rights of first refusal. In short, your visit to the clerk's office may provide you with valuable information[23] about the property. In addition, you may learn important things about the owner—for example, what he bought the property for, the amount of his equity, the pressure (if any) on him from high-interest mortgages or involuntary liens—all of which information can improve your chances of successfully negotiating with the owner.

Opportunities for the Creative Player

The information base in the clerk's and other municipal offices can be the source of "scores" for the creative real estate player.

Finding Property

Not all property available for sale is offered through the brokerage community. In fact there is good property available in every community which can be bought if the seller is identified and found and, the right price offered.

Too many brokers wait for prospective sellers to come to them. Some real estate players go out and look for sellers. Sometimes sellers can be found or created—at very good prices.

Several players I know will drive around a community looking for properties which might coincide with their game plan. Then they go to the clerk's or other municipal offices to locate the owner. Next, they research the owner's situation. Armed with this information, they call the owner and ask if he'd be interested in selling, hoping to negotiate a very favorable purchase. Perhaps one out of 20 such inquiries leads to any thing, but every so often a "score"[24] is made and the player is soon back on the street and in the clerk's office.

"Let me introduce myself..."

One of the most creative real estate players I know is a man I'll call Mr. Harris. Mr. Harris is a self-taught title expert, with a good sense of real estate law.

Mr. Harris spends his days in the municipal offices of various cities looking for "lost" properties, usually undeveloped land on which nobody is paying taxes. The reason for the absence of taxation is usually that the city tax collector can't figure out who owns the land. Harris then begins his homework, researching the title of the land back as far as he can (often into the late 1700s and early 1800s) to find the last recorded owner of the land. Once he gets a name, he goes to the probate courts and attempts to trace this deceased individual's descendants.[25] His objective is to find someone living somewhere in the world who has a claim (no matter how tenuous) to the last recorded owner's estate. Then he makes a phone call:

Harris:	"Do I have Mr. Jack Jones of Albuquerque, New Mexico? Mr. Jones, let me introduce myself. I am Mr. Harry Harris of Boston, Massachusetts. If I were to offer you $1,000 for a deed to land here in Massachusetts to which you may have a claim, what would you say?"
Jones:	"I don't own anything in Massachusetts. I've always lived in New Mexico, as did my father before me."
Harris:	"What about your grandfather?"
Jones:	"I don't know where he was from— somewhere in New England."
Harris:	"Was his name Elias Jones?"
Jones:	"Yes, it was."
Harris:	"Well, Mr. Jones, I'm in the business of taking fliers and while I don't think there's much to it, I'm willing to gamble that your great-grandfather may have owned land in Massachusetts and that you, as one of his

descendants, may have a claim to that land, for which claim I'm prepared to pay you $1,000. Are you interested?"

Jones: "Sure, why not."[26]

Most people in Jones' position take the money—why not, they didn't know they owned the property anyway. And Harris is very good at making the whole thing seem very "iffy," which it often is.

Harris then has Jones sign a Quit-Claim Deed to him and brings a suit in court[27] attempting to establish himself as the legal owner of the land. Whereas these lawsuits may take some time and entail certain notice and publication requirements,[28] there's almost never anyone around to object. So, Harris picks himself up a piece of land for $1,000. Sometimes it's just a sliver, worth little more than Harris paid. *But* sometimes Harris "scores"—buying land for next to nothing which he then resells at an enormous profit.

Notes to Chapter 7

1.   The exact name of the seller, or more accurately the exact name the seller used when he took legal title is critical; for otherwise, the "chain of title" will be broken.

2.   The buyer may take title in the names of friends (whom he trusts); in his attorney's name, as trustee; in the names of different partnerships which he controls; or in different trade names. (In Connecticut a buyer may file a trade name certificate in the town in which the real estate is located such that nobody else may use that name; then, instead of taking title as Sam Jones, he can take title as One Main Street Enterprises (or any other name he creates) solely for the purpose of acquiring one piece of real estate.)

3.   Once a neighborhood suspects that there may be an assemblage occurring, prices go up, for people assume that their piece is essential to the buyer.

4.   Conversely, a real estate player who "stole" a property in an area may deliberately disclose the price to prepare adjoining property owners for his "low ball" offers.

5.   Notwithstanding this nondisclosure, a person knowledgeable in conveyancing can still learn the sales price of a transfer by checking the amount of conveyance tax paid by the seller. Still, most people won't or don't know how to do this and thus the sales price, if not included in the deed, won't usually reach the public's attention.

6.   A description of the perimeters of the property; for example: "Commencing at a monument on the northeast corner of the intersection of Main and Elm Streets and then proceeding 85 feet NW 12 degress 44 feet 33 inches to a point...."

7.   The property address alone (if there is one) is not usually sufficient.

8.   The time to make this inquiry is *before* the closing—either before contract or after contract but with some type of survey contingency in the contract (e.g., "buyer's obligation is hereby made contingent on his receiving a survey to his reasonable satisfaction within seven days of the date of this contract").

9.   If you have any question as to the property lines, you should accompany the surveyor when he does his survey and ask him to show you or to "stake" any uncertain property lines.

10. Not too long ago I was retained by a man who had a serious problem: he had purchased a beautiful home with a new tennis court (built by his seller) but had never properly reviewed the legal description or obtained a survey. He was certainly surprised to subsequently learn that 90% of the tennis court was on his neighbor's property.

11. The signer of the deed is the "grantor," the recipient is the "grantee."

12. The grantor may have long since moved away or may have no assets.

13. This review means more than just identifying the existence of rights or encumbrances. It also entails getting a copy of the written document which defines the right/encumbrance, and examining the specific nature, location and duration of the right/encumbrance.

14. Some rights and encumbrances have a time limit.

15. A good real estate contract or escrow agreement will protect the buyer in the event that the seller grants or is subjected to an encumbrance between the contract date and the closing date.

16. You may recall that we discussed an analogous situation as to rights of first refusal. In that situation, a property owner might grant Jones a right of first refusal in a document which Jones never records. Then, along comes Smith who (with no knowledge of Jones' right of first refusal) buys the property, the owner/seller never having given Jones the opportunity to exercise his right of first refusal. Jones sues Smith claiming that Smith doesn't have good title in light of Jones' unexercised right of first refusal. Who wins? *Smith.* Jones should have recorded the documents granting the right of first refusal so that the world would have known about it.

17. A claim against real estate to secure (an allegation of) money due the claimant. An attachment usually coincides with the commencement of a lawsuit.

18. A *lis pendens* (Latin for "thing pending") is a notice to the world that someone else has claim to an ownership right in the real estate. As to involuntary liens, such as the *lis pendens* and attachment, there are prescribed procedures which must be followed before these documents can be recorded against someone's property. Such procedures prevent an aggressive claimant (with no real lawful claim) from "holding up" a property owner—preventing a sale or refinance—by recording an involuntary lien against the property.

19. The word "lien" is often used to describe any recorded encumbrance.

20. This is usually done by going to the tax assessor's office and finding out when the current owner acquired the property. Sometimes the tax assessor will even have the volume and page of the deed into the current owner. If not, you locate the deed by checking the grantee index (remember, when the current owner first received the deed, he was the *grantee*) around the time of the transfer. Without much trouble you should find the owner listed as the grantee and obtain the volume and page of the deed into him.

21. Sometimes the mortgage deed will include information about the note, such as the interest rate and at times a copy of the note will even be attached to the mortgage deed.

22. Sometimes leases or notices of lease (which indicate leasehold interests in a property) are recorded.

23. Usually also available at the clerk's or nearby municipal offices are recorded surveys, zoning and building permits, tax information, etc.

24. A "score" does not necessarily mean that the player "steals" the property (buys under market) for simply by avoiding a broker, the player may save 5% to 10% off the top of the probable sales price.

25. Once Harris gets the name of the last recorded owner, he checks probate records, digs through newspaper articles, talks to people, etc. in an attempt to find living descendants.

26. Jones might ask for more specifics, but Harris is always evasive. He figures that he's done all the work and he's not going to let Jones capitalize on his discovery.

27. Either an action to quiet title or a declaratory judgment. Sometimes, rather than bring a lawsuit, Harris will attempt to

convince a title insurance company to insure the chain of title into him. If the chain looks good, the title insurers will sometimes do so.

28. Saying to the world: "Harris is claiming title to this land. Anybody object?"

8
Participants in the Game

Attorneys

Although it is hazardous to generalize about the members of any profession, I do have some very definite opinions about most attorneys and their role in the real estate game.[1]

Attorneys are trained to analyze a situation and look for (and hopefully protect against) problems which may arise. This training includes the reading of thousands of cases (reports of lawsuits) which arose because of problems in business dealings, problems which could not be solved between the parties themselves. While the ratio of normal business dealings to problems might be 100 to one and the ratio of business problems to law suits might be 10 to one, the attorney learns and trains on these 1,000 to one situations. The result is that some attorneys become too "problem sensitive:" they lose their overview and ability to analyze risk objectively.[2] For this reason, a real estate player must be careful in dealing with attorneys—not only the other party's but his own as well.

Some lawyers may also view you, the client, as a potential problem. They fear that they may make a mistake which will cost you money and that you will bring a malpractice action against them. Thus they review a business situation *doubly* cautiously—not only to protect you vis-a-vis the other party or parties in the transaction, but also to protect themselves vis-a-vis you.

The point is to use and control your attorney—and not be controlled by him. I have seen many situations in which a real estate player wanted very much to pursue a property but dropped or lost the deal when his attorney advised him against it or otherwise "killed" it. The player's mistake was in letting himself and the deal be controlled by his attorney. This can be a critical error.

Needless to say, you should always consider your attorney's advice. But in doing so also be sensitive to his orientation:

Is he overly conservative?

Is he risk adverse?

Is he envious of your success?

Is he one who believes that people should earn their money gradually and that quick, big hits (scores) are unnatural?

It is certainly important for you to listen to your attorney, but at the same time, be aware of his general business perspective and how that may (consciously or subconsciously) influence his advice.

I also suggest that while you should inquire as to your attorney's opinions on the deal in general, you should weigh much more heavily his counsel on the legal issues involved. Everyone likes to give advice and while it is helpful to listen to different points of view, you must have confidence in your own analysis of the business end of a deal. Do not be intimidated by a lot of fancy looking diplomas. They represent a specialized training in one area—the law. They do not indicate a thing about your lawyer's general business judgment. While he may be very free with nonlegal advice, his own investment record may be very ordinary.

Lawyers also have big egos. This comes from giving advice all day long. Asked their opinion all day long, day in and day out, some lawyers begin to think they have something great to say on almost any subject. So, sooner or later some (many?) attorneys develop big egos and as a result don't like to play a secondary or subordinate role in a business deal. But, this is exactly their role in a real estate play. They work for you, the real estate player. A good attorney can be a very valuable ally, but you are the chairman of the board. It's you who is investing the time, energy and money. It's you who stands to win or lose. It's you who is taking the risk. It's you who pays his bills.

Pick an attorney carefully. Do a lot of asking around. Satisfied (or dissatisfied) clients are a great source of information. Ask about a lawyer's knowledge of the real estate game and about his integrity. Ask about his billing—is he reasonable? Also, ask about his accessibility; it does you no good to have the world's greatest attorney if he has no time for you.

Then, have a get-acquainted meeting. Explain to him your view on attorneys and how you plan *"to use him"* in your real estate transactions. Do his eyes start to flash anger? If so, you may be hiring a potential ego problem, one who is extremely intelligent and knowledgeable but who won't be able to take a back seat to you. One who may flex his muscles and kill a deal (in your "best" interest, of course) that you really should have made. While I do not believe that a lawyer will do anything to deliberately hurt you, a lawyer who cannot psychologically sit in the "back seat" begins to handle the deal as if it were his, operating (perhaps subconsciously) as *he* thinks appropriate and maybe (if, for example, he is very risk adverse) in a way which kills the deal because *he (not you)*feels it is too risky.

A lawyer can kill a deal in any one of ten different ways. For example, as your lawyer alone generally communicates with the other party's attorney, he can do things which he believes to be in your best interest but which may work against you. For example, in negotiating a contract he can demand too much by way of legal protection and thus antagonize the other attorney. He can characterize certain contract clauses as "deal-breakers" in an attempt to get you the tightest document possible and in so doing convey the (inaccurate) image that *you* are a hardliner and that negotiation and compromise with you will be difficult. Or, he can draft a 20-page lease, where a 10-page lease would do, in an attempt to protect you against every possible problem that has ever occurred in the history of landlord-tenant relations.[3] Unfortunately, when the prospective tenant's lawyer gets the 20-page lease, he may perceive *you* as a nitpicker or overaggressive, or just someone who will be difficult to deal with.[4] And, once the other party's attorney gets a negative impression (even though inaccurate) of you, trouble can begin for this attorney is often the eyes and ears of his client once the preliminary negotiations move into the documents stage. Accordingly, if he comes to the conclusion that "[you] are going to be very difficult to deal with" his client may be scared off and the deal ruined. And all because you were unable to control *your own* attorney.

Once you have established a relationship with a good attorney, treat him well, for he is a very important part of your team and his performance can have a lot to do with your eventual success. Even though he's been able to subordinate his ego to your running of the show, presume he nevertheless has a good-sized ego and play to it:

"Wow, did you do a great job in pulling that deal off!"

"I could never have done this closing without your help."

"That idea you had made all the difference."

These five-second comments will really be appreciated and will emphasize to your attorney his importance to you. Everyone works harder when appreciated and your gratitude will go a long way toward establishing a long-term, beneficial relationship with someone who may become a trusted friend and adviser.

Lastly, always pay your attorney quickly and in full. He's in business, too, and his billings are his source of income. Your prompt payment will insure his quick response when you need him; nothing is worse than trying to get your attorney's assistance in an emergency, when you owe him money. Also, payment is another expression of your appreciation for his work; to some people it speaks louder than words and nobody objects to being paid too quickly. Finally, be aware that as your success grows, your attorney cannot help but be a little envious. He may see you make $100,000 on a deal for which you pay him a $5,000 legal fee—and your time and effort invested may be no greater than his. He naturally will be upset if you delay in paying or, haggle over the amount of, the fee.

Bankers

We discussed in Chapter 3 how important it is to develop a good working relationship with a bank and a banker within that bank. This relationship will be one of your most valuable assets when playing the real estate game.

Be aggressive in your attempt to develop a good banking relationship. Even if you are a new customer to a bank, actively push to get to the right person (people) within the bank. Few things more consistently kill good deals than an unimaginative, conservative banker. Be especially careful of the mid-level banker who has decided to stay with banking for life and is very afraid of a screw-up which might hurt his tenure. These individuals always find several reasons not to finance a deal with anything more than absolute minimum risk. As a player, all of your deals will involve some element of risk. If you get stuck with a "mid-level lifer," your chances of getting creative or aggressive financing are very slim.

Seek out the right banker just as you do the right deal—with persistence and energy. Don't settle. And, once the right relationship is started, work to strengthen and develop it. Finally, never assume that the relationship is forever. Good bankers are always looking around, perhaps to get into a profession which pays better than (traditionally low-paying) banking. Good senior-level bankers may move into a different area within the bank, may move to a different bank, or may move up the executive ladder to a point where you lose easy access to them. Therefore, once you begin to form a good relationship with the right person, ask him to introduce you to other key people within the bank. In this way, you leverage your contact with one person into a relationship with several of the key people within the bank, and insure against a disruption in the flow of financing in the event of personnel changes within the bank.

Brokers

Brokers, as a profession, have bad P.R. If you haven't already heard, sooner or later you will hear:

"I have no use for brokers."

"Brokers are all sharks."[5]

"Son of a gun wants a 6% commission for *doing nothing!*"

There are, of course, unethical brokers, but in large part I believe the negative P.R. arises due to reasons other than their general level of integrity:

1. Brokers are middlemen; therefore it's sometimes hard for principals to perceive or acknowledge the role the broker plays in a deal.

2. A broker may work on 50 deals for every one he makes. Therefore, while his commission may seem inequitable or excessive in light of the time and energy he invests in the one deal which closes, it may in fact be underpayment given the totality of his effort on a particular property or, in general.

3. When a good deal (everything from a well-priced house to a great commercial property) comes along, brokers must move quickly in an effort to get their customers to the deal first—remember only one broker will make the selling commission. In the rush they sometimes act rudely and aggressively.

4. In general, there are a lot of brokers around—it's a very competitive business. To get the listing or the customers, or to make the deals, good brokers by necessity must be a bit pushy.

5. Brokers are easily cheated by principals who are determined to avoid them. A seller can wait until a listing expires and attempt to beat a broker by subsequently deal ing with the broker's prospect. Or, a buyer can go to a seller (after being shown a property by a broker) and negotiate directly, the two of them collaborating to beat the broker and save a commission.[6]

The point is that brokers as a whole are no more or less ethical than members of any other profession. The nature of their business requires them to act aggressively at times and, on occasion, it appears that they make excessive commissions doing very little. The truth is that brokers must be aggressive in order to succeed and that very few brokers get rich by brokering alone.

Good brokerage relationships are very important to a real estate player. Day after day brokers have their ear to the ground and sooner or later one of them will come up with a good deal. When they do, you want to be the first person they call.

When a broker does discover a good deal he has to move quickly in an effort to make the sale before some other broker does. Therefore, to avoid wasting time, he must introduce the deal only to those individuals whom he believes can act quickly. That is, he won't call you first unless he believes in your knowledge (he can't wait for you to educate yourself), your financial strength, and your decisiveness.

Our company has worked hard at developing a reputation among the commercial brokers in our area for being strong, capable, and quick to act. When a broker calls us with our type of deal, and so long as it hasn't been "shopped,"[8] we always look at it immediately and give him a very quick response. In this way, in the event that the deal isn't for us, we don't delay the broker. And, if it is for us, by moving in a hurry we increase our chances of getting the deal (and, of the broker earning a commission).

In return, we want a broker to call us first and give us a little lead time. We don't want to be one of five calls such that we find ourselves working against four other players within the first hour of receiving the broker's call. While it may make sense for a broker to hedge his bet by calling several players at once, we prefer not to work with this type of broker. All we ask for is the first call and, one day lead time.

As with attorneys and bankers, a good relationship with a hustling, savvy broker can be very important. Look to develop several good brokerage relationships; the result will be a pipeline to the best deals around. As with all the members of your team, treat your brokers well. Be particularly sensitive to how they make their money and try to see that they make a lot of money from or through you.[9]

Notes to Chapter 8

1.   A very small percentage of attorneys are also real estate players.

2.   Risk, by definition, includes both an upside and a downside. But lawyers generally only get involved when the negative side of a risk arises: when their banker client calls to institute a foreclosure, or when their builder client calls to initiate a mechanic's lien, or when their landlord client calls with tenant problems. Sooner or later attorneys lose their perspective on risk and become overcautious.

3.   He may also be attempting to protect himself against you (malpractice) in the event something goes wrong which leads to a lawsuit—and which situation (even if one in a million) is covered in his 20- but not his 10-page lease.

4.   Conversely, some real estate players use their attorneys in a bad guy/good guy kind of game. They instruct the attorney to come on real hard and put as much in the contract/lease as possible. If the negotiation then gets heated, the player steps in, mitigates the situation and looks like a hero. In this way the player may win points with the other party, blaming the entire probelm on "the lawyers."

5.   Other words are also common.

6.   A listing agreement should protect a broker against these possibilities; the point is that the ease with which they can be cheated sometimes forces them to act in an untrusting and hard-line manner.

7.   Sometimes a broker will get an exclusive (e.g. a listing of a house for sale or a property for lease or, an agreement with a tenant that the tenant will work with no other broker) such that he's guaranteed at least a portion of the commission. Still (as an exclusive agent is at the least morally obligated to push a listing to all brokers within the community and, show a tenant all available properties for lease), the exclusive broker will often act in a manner (sometimes quickly) designed to sell/lease the listed property to one of *his* customers or, place *his* exclusive tenant in one of his landlord client's buildings, in an effort to earn the entire commission available.

8.   Offered to several other potential purchasers.

9.   Some players who hear of a deal from an "outside broker" will call their own broker and ask him to follow up on the deal in an effort to get their broker the selling commission. Whether or not you choose to adopt this practice, a general loyalty to your broker will be much appreciated.

9

The Art of Persuasion

An important skill for success in the real estate game is the ability to persuade others to act as you'd like them to, be it in convincing a seller to sell, a lender to finance, a tenant to lease, or a buyer to buy.[1] Included under the heading of persuasion is negotiation—the interplay of two (or more) people, each attempting to structure a deal more to his favor than to that of the other party (parties).

Some people are born salesmen. Others can learn techniques which, when intermixed with their own personality, will improve their ability to "sell."[2] Before discussing technique, however, I think it is critical to state my overview as to the art of persuasion/selling.

In my opinion, the great sellers don't try to convince a buyer to accept the seller's point of view, but instead tailor their sale *to the buyer's point of view*. In other words, a great seller will try to get inside the buyer's head, identify the buyer's needs and/or desires, and attempt to persuade the buyer that what is being sold coincides and dovetails with the buyer's needs/desires.

There is a great deal of literature on the subject of persuasion. Although each author describes the process with different words,[3] the *key*, in my opinion, is always the same—*you must not attempt to sell; you must instead attempt to*

165

induce the buyer to buy. The difference is not semantics, the difference is approach. Work on the sale *not* from your side of the table but rather from the buyer's side; let him reach across the table to take your idea—don't push it at him. In my opinion, no matter what the situation, keeping this overview in mind at all times can mean the difference between the success or failure of your persuasion.

Now, on to some ideas about preparation and technique:

Do Your Homework

It is critical that you be 100% informed and conversant in the relevant facts of a deal—before even attempting to sell. The informed seller not only makes a much more fluid presentation, but also is better able to react to the other party's comments, questions or tactics. Nothing can kill a great sales pitch more quickly than a comment from the buyer for which the seller has no intelligent response:

Buyer: "Well, all that makes sense but have you considered the new tax rule on noninterest-bearing loans?"

UNPREPARED Seller: "Uh...no, but..." (To himself: what new tax rule?)

PREPARED Seller: "Yes I have. In fact, if you'll recall what I said earlier...."

Your response to the buyer's question (if prepared) will not only maintain the momentum of your presentation but also will impress him with your knowledge and thoroughness.

Prepare Your Pitch Before You Open Your Mouth

I am constantly amazed at the number of people who ad-lib their persuasion. This makes absolutely no sense. You only get so much of another person's open-minded attention. Take advantage of it. Think through what points you want to make and do your best to make them.

Stick to the Track—Don't Ramble.

Once you know what you're going to say, stick to the script as much as possible. Needless to say, there will be many situations when you have to react to the comments and questions of the "persuadee" but, hopefully, you've anticipated these points and thought through your answers. Whereas you obviously cannot be rigid, neither should you ramble. Besides losing the persuadee's interest, you may inadvertently give away information about your position.

Conversely, I am always happy when the other party starts rambling. By listening very carefully I sometimes pick up comments which reveal something about the other party's situation. In a competitive situation like a tough negotiation, you may come out the winner if you know one or two things more about the other party's position than he knows about yours.

I'm not advising you to sit quietly in a room and discuss only your prearranged points. But when you do just talk, go off on meaningless tangents—the weather, sports, politics. Never free-flow on anything relevant to the deal being negotiated.

Try to Control the Discussion

I believe that your chances of successfully persuading someone are greatly increased when you are able to control the flow and momentum of the discussion. In doing so, you must be sensitive to where you do and don't want the negotiation to go.

For example, before making a pitch, I always try to identify my weak spots. Then, during the meeting I try very hard to keep the discussion away from these danger areas. By listening carefully, you can often sense when the other party is heading in a direction which could end up in a danger area. When that begins to happen, I try to use what the other party is saying as a stepping stone in an effort to turn the discussion toward something logically connected to what he was saying—but away from the danger area. If you are lucky, the other party will forget his original train of thought and not wander back toward the danger area.

You must, of course, be careful when using this technique. If you are too obvious, your effort may backfire and the other party may realize that he's on to something. Then, you may be the reason that he focuses on an area that you didn't even want to discuss.

Let me give you an example. Suppose you are attempting to negotiate the purchase of a small office building which you intend to renovate. As part of your proposal to the seller, you are requesting that he take back a purchase-money mortgage to be subordinated to a first mortgage placed against the property at closing. Whereas you are willing to negotiate the terms of this mortgage, what you really want is freedom of subordination, that is, the ability to obtain as large a first mortgage and thereby overfinance the deal. You know from prior discussions with the seller[4] that conceptually he has no problem with the idea of a subordinated (second) purchase-money mortgage. What you don't know are his thoughts[5] on the *amount* of the first mortgage that he'll subordinate to.[6]

So, your game plan going into the negotiation with the seller is that while you will, of course, try for as many of the items of your purchase package as possible (price; closing date; amount on contract; rate, term and amount of the purchase-money mortgage),[7] your number one priority is to keep the seller from focusing on the amount of the first mortgage which he will have to subordinate to at closing[8]—this is your danger area.[9]

In this negotiation you must be sensitive to the seller's train of thought and keep him away from a discussion of a limit on the first mortgage. If the discussion begins to move in that direction, you must attempt to divert the flow—to a related but non-dangerous area.

For example, let's say that the discussion is proceeding as follows:

YOU (PERSUADOR): "Well, I guess that I can live with a rate of 14% (on the purchase-money mortgage), but I really need your help with the term—I'd like 10 years."

SELLER (PERSUADEE): "I don't know Mr. Buyer; I'm 60 years old and I'd like to get repaid in full sooner than 10 years."

PERSUADOR: "I understand but I will be paying off a certain amount of your loan every year, so that there won't be much actual debt left in the last years of the loan."

SELLER (THINKING): "Yes, I see that. What by the way will be the term of your first mortgage?"

NOTE: BEWARE! SELLER'S THOUGHT PROCESS MAY BE LEADING TO THE DANGER AREA (I.E. THE FIRST MORTGAGE)

PERSUADOR #1 (NOT USING HIS HEAD): "Well, probably 15 years but I haven't really settled with my banker on all the terms of the first mortgage."

MISTAKE: PERSUADOR #1 SHOULD HAVE TURNED THE DISCUSSION AWAY FROM THE TERMS OF THE FIRST MORTGAGE.

SELLER (THINKING): "Well, maybe 10 years is reasonable. By the way, where do you plan to get your first mortgage?"

DANGER! GET OFF THIS LINE OF DISCUSSION!

PERSUADOR #1 (NOT THINKING): "Constitution Federal. They're a very good lender; they almost always give me everything I ask for." DUMB!

CONTRAST:

PERSUADOR #2 (THINKING): "I haven't even thought about it...[smiling sadly] all these darn lenders are so tough these days and the bureaucracy is crazy. I don't know how you feel, but it seems that our whole country is becoming one big bureaucracy."[10]

SMART: AT LEAST PERSUADOR #2 HAS MADE AN EFFORT TO CHANGE THE SUBJECT.

SELLER TO PERSUADOR #1: "Oh, what kind of first mortgage do you think you'll get?" DANGER! DANGER!

PERSUADOR 1 (*FINALLY* THINKING): "To tell you the truth, I'm really not sure. You know they tell you one thing and then end up doing another. I can't stand that—if people would just tell you right from the start they can't help you, it would save everybody a lot of time. Don't you think?"

This effort by PERSUADOR #1 to turn the subject, albeit late, is a good one, for he has said several things which may catch SELLER'S interest and divert his train of thought: banks mislead you; people say one thing and mean another (ironic?); people waste your time. If PERSUADOR #1 is lucky, SELLER will respond to PERSUADOR #1's question—"Don't you think?"—and perhaps get off on one of these tangents.

If however, PERSUADOR #1 is not lucky, SELLER'S train of thought may continue:

SELLER: "Constitution Federal sounds better than my bank. By the way, what size first mortgage have they offered you?"

The danger area has been entered because now the SELLER can't help but focus on the amount in front of his mortgage. PERSUADOR #1 should have been more sensitive to the flow of his conversation with SELLER and tried to divert the discussion long before it got to this point.

One last reminder: remember that while this technique can be helpful in keeping a negotiation away from your danger areas, you must attempt to divert the discussion only with a natural segue or transition. Otherwise, what you're trying to do may be too obvious with the result that you highlight rather than avoid the danger area.

Stay in Character

Without sacrificing sincerity, try to stay within the character you've decided has the best chance to succeed with the persuasion. If polite but aloof is more likely to win for you, try to discipline yourself to stay with this approach. If you are a naturally gregarious person, that's great, but it may not always be the best posture in, for example, a difficult negotiation. Therefore, even when just chatting with the other party, try to stay in the mold you've set for it's difficult to move back and forth into different personalities as the subject matter of the meeting changes.

For example, when confronted with a hard-nosed guy across the table, I always try to be friendly and start the meeting off by finding a subject—irrelevant to the deal—about which he has a great interest. If I'm lucky and hit on some thing he likes to talk about, the change in his attitude can be amazing. Recently I went to lunch with one of our tenants the purpose of which was to negotiate a new lease. I knew that the tenant was a tough customer and I anticipated a difficult negotiation. But before I would let the discussion turn to business (it's usually easier to delay at a meal because there's always a lot of small talk when ordering), I searched for a subject about which the tenant might be interested. I got lucky and hit on golf (about which I know very little). For 45 minutes we talked golf (the tenant was a fanatic) and the change in the tenant's attitude was remarkable. Whereas we began lunch as two business adversaries, 45 minutes later we were golfing buddies trading war stories. As a result, he felt better about me, dropped his armor just a bit, and in the last 10 minutes of lunch we discussed the lease and reached an amicable agreement.

Since my golfing friend may someday read this book, I want to say on the record that the new lease was fair for both of us. My point is that by moving him out of an adversarial posture, I believe that I increased the chances of he and I reaching an agreement.

Make People Like You

This technique is so simplistic it almost sounds silly to mention. Nevertheless, I can't believe how many people don't operate in this fashion. The rule is very simple: make the persuadee like you as a person and you are much more likely to get what you want.

No matter what your true feelings about the persuadee, no matter what character you may be playing, no matter on which side of the bed you got up that morning, *always* make an effort to get the persuadee to like and feel good about you. It's elementary that no one wants to see (and certainly not advance) the success of someone they don't like. On the other hand, everyone feels good about helping someone they really do like. It's human nature.

Making someone like you is not easy: in fact those who have the ability are very lucky. If there is such a thing as a technique, I call it the "chameleon approach." A chameleon is an animal that changes color to blend in with its surroundings. Similarly, the individual who can blend in with any type of person (in other words, who can make the persuadee feel that the persuador is just like him) has the greatest chance of getting that person to like him. In my opinion, this chameleon quality comes most naturally to someone who really likes other people and is happy and comfortable adapting himself to their styles and interests. This individual is usually self-effacing and doesn't take himself too seriously. A chameleon can be a great and disarming negotiator; before you know it, you're actually subconsciously rooting for the other guy!

Subtlety and Misdirection are 100 Times Better Than Table Pounding

I believe that selling is most effective when done softly, almost subliminally. The great salespeople sneak up on you; subconsciously you're being convinced of something and you may not even know it. Great salespeople use an approach also used by magicians—misdirection. Misdirection is conduct by a magician which makes you focus on something (for example, his right hand), while everything important is going on somewhere else (for example, his left hand). By the time you figure out (if ever) what's happened, it's too late; you've been fooled (sold?). Similarly, a great salesperson (let's use, as an example, an automobile salesman) comes at you indirectly, not talking only to what you anticipate (e.g. price, warranty, extras) but also to all those sub- and semiconscious impulses which cause us to act (for example, pride, ego, insecurity). Before you know it, the discussion is not about the automobile but: (1) the disgrace of wastefulness—he's trying to sell you a gas efficient car; (2) the importance of a good appearance—he's trying to sell you a prestige automobile; (3) girls/boys—he's trying to sell you a sports car. And the great salespeople are so indirect and natural that you forget about buying the car and have a 10-minute discussion on the subject (e.g. appearance, sex, prestige) which is, at least in part, behind your desire to buy. By the time you get back to considering the purchase, your mind is pretty well made up.

In my opinion, the effective way to employ this technique is to attempt to identify in advance of a negotiation the persuadee's soft spots—the reasons which motivate him to act.[11] For example, suppose you want to buy a small apartment building owned by a 70-year-old seller. You learn from the broker that the seller is considering retirement. You also know from seeing the building that it is management intensive, yet too small to economically justify a full-time manager. You therefore assume that a major reason the building is for sale is that the seller is tired of handling tenant calls and problems; you guess that the seller's motivation is to simplify and depressurize his life. Your problem is that you can't afford the asking price.

You ask the broker to set up a meeting with you and the seller. Your goal is to come away from this meeting with a deal.[12] Your game plan is to play to what you believe to be the seller's motivation for selling—to simplify his life. You're a good salesperson and you know that your effort must be indirect and casual.

YOU: "Glad to meet you, Mr. Seller, I'm Joe Smith."

SELLER: "Nice to meet you."

YOU: "Before we talk about your property, I just wanted to tell you a little about myself, just so you'll know who you're dealing with."

SELLER: "Fine."

NOW YOU HAVE A MINUTE TO TALK—TO IGNITE CERTAIN THOUGHT PROCESSES WITHIN THE SELLER'S MIND.

> YOU: "I'm 24 years *old* with a lot of *energy* and desire."

YOU'VE MENTIONED TWO IMPORTANT TOPICS: AGE AND ENERGY. MAYBE SELLER IS SUBCONSCIOUSLY COMPARING HIS OWN CONDITION TO YOURS.

> YOU: "I know that owning an apartment building is a *lot of work*, but I've got *plenty of time* and *very strong legs*."

THAT SENTENCE TOOK YOU FIVE TO 10 SECONDS TO SAY, YET IT MAY BE THE KEY WHICH UNLOCKS THE SELLER'S RESOLVE AGAINST DROPPING HIS PRICE FOR NOW HE CAN'T HELP BUT BEGIN TO THINK ABOUT HIS MOTIVATION FOR SELLING.

> YOU: "My goal is to acquire as much real estate as I can in the next 20 years or so, *work as hard* as possible and then [smiling] hopefully *retire* and *enjoy life* a bit."

IF YOUR MANNER HAS BEEN CASUAL AND FRIENDLY, YOU'VE NOW GOT SELLER WHERE YOU WANT HIM—BEFORE THE DISCUSSION EVEN TURNS TO PRICE.

With this technique, as with many of the others, preparation is important. Don't ad-lib if you can help it. Find out what you can about the persuadee and try to analyze what will motivate him to act in the direction you seek. Then, when meeting with him, play to these motivations, with the aim of directing his thought processes to the points on which you want him to focus.

Never Talk Too Fast

In my opinion, an error many people make unconsciously, is speaking too quickly. Intrinsically, there is nothing wrong with speaking at a rapid pace; it's just that most of us have a negative image of fast talking salespeople. The impression is that they are slimy, shyster types even though in reality they may be very ethical people. This reaction to "fast talkers" may simply be the result of television and movie caricatures, but the fact remains that most people are put on the defensive by rapid-fire sales pitches.

Therefore, in making your persuasion, make a conscious effort to speak at a moderate, even pace. If you are one of those people whose mind races ahead of your speech, don't try to catch your words up to your thoughts. Hopefully, you'll remember all the points you want to make but even if you don't, speaking too rapidly may mean losing the sale—not on the merits but rather on the presentation. As discussed below, at times packaging—the way you present your points—is more important than the product itself.

Packaging is Critical

Under the heading of packaging, there are some other important rules:

Dress to Make the Persuadee Comfortable

Your apparel may be right out of *Gentleman's Quarterly*, but if the persuadee is a person who just doesn't dress that way, your sharp appearance may work against you. Perhaps the persuadee will have trouble warming up to you, feeling that your respective attire is tangible evidence of the differences between the two of you. Perhaps he will be intimidated by you in a situation where you want cooperation, not awe.

As another example, if you are a very casual dresser and you are meeting with your banker, you may wish to dress "conservative" so as to help your banker feel comfortable with you. The point is to use your dress and appearance as part of your overall persuasion.

Pick the Place of the Meeting Carefully

Where are you most likely to convince the persuadee? Your office? His? Common ground? Think it through. Where will the persuadee feel most intimidated (if that's the effect you're shooting for)? Most comfortable (if that's what you want)? Most impressed? And so on.

Once you've identified the game plan of your presentation, you will know what impression you want to give the persuadee. Then, set the stage. Where is the play most likely to run successfully? That's where your meeting should be.

Sometimes Staged Events Can Be Persuasive

Once I was trying to sell one of our smaller buildings. A meeting with the prospective purchaser was to occur in my office. Although there were several reasons why we had chosen to sell the building, the impression that I wanted to create in the purchaser's mind was that I was too busy with bigger matters to be bothered with this building and that it was only because he was catching me at a time when I was particularly hassled, that I'd consider selling at such a reasonable price.

Accordingly, before the meeting I told my secretary to put all incoming calls through to me, even though I would normally hold calls during a meeting. During the discussion with the prospective buyer there must have been 10 interruptions for "important" phone calls.

> ME: "I'm sorry for the interruptions but now at least you can see why I'm selling this smaller deal."

> PROSPECTIVE BUYER (TO HIMSELF): "Boy am I in the right place at the right time."

Work the Crowd

Although I prefer to go one-on-one with a persuadee, many of them will bring their broker or lawyer to a meeting. Rather than letting these people bother me, I try to use them to my advantage. For example, if a seller brings his lawyer, play to the lawyer's ego by asking his advice or opinions on legal questions which have no effect one way or another on the negotiation. Or, perhaps, spotlight his knowledge by asking him to confirm information which you already know to be true.

> YOU: "I'm not sure but I believe the zoning rule in this town requires 10 parking spaces. Is that correct, Mr. Lawyer?"

By involving him in the easy stuff and making him look good, you may find that he drops his defenses a bit, so that he's less adversarial or attentive when you get into the real meat of your proposal.

The point of "packaging" is that sometimes the style of the presentation is as critical as the substance. Be sensitive to the whole drama—don't focus on just the oral portion of your presentation. Your objective should be to create an overall impression which will induce the persuadee to either consciously or subconsciously act in the manner you'd like. Keep in mind that there are many forces which cause us to act; some we're in touch with, others we're not. Play to each persuadee as a unique individual with all sorts of impulses and motivations influencing his decisions. And, through your presentation, attempt to activate those impulses which will cause the persuadee to realize that his needs/desires really do coincide with the terms of your proposal!

Win the Persuadee's Trust with "Giveaways."

Many persuadees will enter a meeting on the defensive, distrustful. I always try to win their trust early in the meeting. One technique is to disclose your "entire" situation, showing that you have nothing to hide. That technique was used on me recently and it was very disarming:

> OTHER GUY: "Jim, maybe I talk too much but here's my exact situation..."

> I (TO MYSELF): "I like this guy. Since he trusts me, I trust him."

Another technique is to illustrate your integrity by revealing some bit of information, which you think the other party probably already knows. For example, if the scuttlebutt is that a new shopping center will be built near the persuadee's land (thereby increasing its value) and you have a pretty good idea that the persuadee has heard the rumors, you might try:

> YOU: "You probably haven't heard about it and I'm speaking against my own interest, but I want you to know that there are rumors that a new shopping center is going in up the street from you."

> PERSUADEE (TO HIMSELF): "Yeah, I heard that, too, but at least the guy's honest enough to bring it up."

Be Sensitive to the Momentum of Your Effort

I believe that every persuasion has a momentum; sometimes it flows your way, sometimes against you. Even if you're doing most of the talking, be very aware of what's going on across the table. Is the persuadee listening? Is he daydreaming? What do his questions or comments indicate? In other words, continually evaluate your performance—how are you doing?

If you feel that you're losing the persuadee, you might consider a radical change in the subject, just to get back his attention.

> YOU (LOOKING OUT THE WINDOW): "Wow! Did you see that car? Must have been a Duesenberg!"

Even if the persuadee has no interest in cars, you may be able to use the interruption (self-created) to break the presentation with a minute or two of chitchat before going back at it from another angle.

Earlier I suggested that you should not ad-lib and should try to stick to the track of your script. What I am suggesting now is not meant to contradict that rule—the great salespeople not only prepare their primary presentation but also several fallbacks in the event approach number one goes nowhere. However, as a last measure, even ad-libbing is better than beating a dead horse (and if you are tuned into the persuadee, you should know when your pitch just isn't working). If you've run out of prepared attacks, what the heck, you might as well ad-lib. While I admit that ad-libbing has worked effectively for me on occasion, I believe that the key was my total familiarity with the deal and the persuadee so that the "ad-lib" was really an informed guess based on homework and preparation. In any event, if you feel yourself losing the persuasion, vary your effort—don't fight the momentum.

You must also be sensitive to the situation when the momentum is going your way. This is the time to let inertia[13] take over and not do or say anything to interrupt the flow. This may sound easy, but I can't count how many times I've seen a good persuasion lost because the salesperson wasn't sensitive to this rule.

Perhaps what happens is that some persuadors do sense things going their way and in the excitement of "victory" forget the rules of momentum. Smelling the "kill," they lose their head and really turn on the razzle-dazzle. For example:

PERSUADOR (TO HIMSELF): "Ahah! You think that idea was good. Wait until you hear this one..."

PERSUADEE (TO HIMSELF): "I hadn't considered that, but I'm not sure it works to my advantage."

OR

PERSUADOR (TO HIMSELF): "Wow, that was a good 10 minutes. He really seemed to like it. Maybe he'd like to hear just a little more."

PERSUADEE (TO HIMSELF): "I wish this guy would quit when he's ahead. Oh gosh, it's 2:00 p.m. I'd better get going. I'll sleep on this and get back to him tomorrow."

Know when you're winning and when to stop talking. Don't let the rush of an apparently successful presentation affect you. In other words, let inertia work *for you*.

Always Keep an Overview

No matter how a meeting may twist and turn, as the persuador, you must *at all times* keep in mind why you're there and what you've got to accomplish. Unlike the persuadee, if you walk out of the meeting with nothing, you've failed in your mission. You do not have the luxuries that the persuadee or anyone else in the meeting has.

Don't Get Angry

If you get angry you're surely going to make less effective use of your time. And your anger will usually initiate or exacerbate similar feelings from the persuadee, so that the chances of his liking you are from then on very slim. You must discipline yourself not to get baited or agitated because, although you may win an argument, you'll most probably lose the war.

Don't Get "Macho" Over Small Points

Don't prove your toughness by fighting over irrelevant or small points. What good does it do to win a couple of small points if the result of the fight is to get only 10% of what you came for? Keep the overview! Forget the small points and concentrate on getting 90% of the important points.

Don't Get Tired or Impatient

Some meetings can last for hours yet the critical decisions may not be made until the last 10 minutes. Don't get worn down or impatient. Outlast the persuadee. Don't give in on key points just to get the meeting over—that's his luxury, not yours.

Concentrate

The persuadee can afford to relax and let his mind wander. You can't. At all times, even in a long meeting, you must be aware of the meeting's flow and do your best to orchestrate it. Even when the discussion has turned to idle chatter you must keep your head: What time did the persuadee say his next meeting was? I'd better get this thing back on track or I won't have time to finish my points.

It is so tempting to relax the mind—especially when that's what everyone else in the room is doing. But, again, this is a luxury which you just don't have when you're the persuador. If you lose the sense of where you are at all times, the result may be failure.

Notes to Chapter 9

1.   There are a lot of middlemen in the real estate game, most notably brokers and lawyers. I believe that when trying to persuade another party, you must deal directly with the principal whenever possible. If you deal only through a middleman, your opportunity to persuade is greatly diminished.

2.   For the remainder of this chapter, "sell" is used in its broadest sense, synonymous with "persuade." Similarly, when I use "buyer" I mean anyone who is the object of a persuasion. I have also made up and use the words "persuador" (seller) and "persuadee" (buyer).

3.   Spencer Johnson and Larry Wilson, *The One Minute Sales Person* (New York: William Morrow and Company, 1984):
   "I never forget that *people hate to be sold but they love to buy.*" (Emphasis is the authors'.)
   "People do things for their own reasons, not ours."
Herb Cohen, *You Can Negotiate Anything* (Secaucus, N.J.: Lyle Stuart, 1980):
   "If you want to persuade people, show the immediate relevance and value of what you're saying in terms of meeting *their needs and desires.*" (Emphasis is the author's.)
Jerry Richardson and Joel Margulis, *The Magic of Rapport* (New York: Avon books, 1981):

"Keep in mind that people do things for *their* reasons, not for yours. *The art of persuasion consists of being able to determine what those reasons are and then presenting your ideas in ways that fit the habitual decision processes of the people you want to influence.*" (Emphasis is the authors'.)

4.   Or from other sources of information, for example, the broker or street talk.

5.   It is also possible that the seller is not too savvy and hasn't even focused on this issue.

6.   Remember, if he takes the position that he will not subordinate to a first mortgage in excess of $X and $X is too low for you, then the whole idea of aggressively financing or overfinancing the deal will not work.

7.   Presumably, from prior discussions you know that the two of you are close on these points.

8.   Your objective is to leave the negotiating room with a general (opaque) agreement from him: "to subordinate his mortgage to your first mortgage." If the contract does not state a specific limit on the first mortgage, I believe that the seller is obligated to subordinate to whatever size first mortgage that you are able to obtain.

9.   It is possible that the seller's attorney may be at this meeting and you must also keep him away from the danger area.

10. Good choice of subject because everybody hates bureaucracies.

11. Remember the overview: YOU DON'T SELL, THE BUYER BUYS!

12. Remember, however, that until you have something in writing you don't have anything that's legally enforceable (Statute of Frauds).

13. "**Inertia**: *the property of matter by which it retains its velocity along a straight line so long as it is not acted upon by an external force.*" The Random House Dictionary of the English Language (Random House: New York, 1966).

10

Entrepreneurship

To some extent every real estate player is an entrepreneur[1] in that a player intermixes risk, capital and effort in an attempt to make a profit. The key element is that the player assumes a risk—not only a financial risk but also a risk of public failure and all the opprobrium that goes with it. The more entrepreneurial you are, the greater the commitment you may wish to make to the real estate game.

There are players who are holding full-time jobs in professions having nothing to do with real estate. There are players who are retired and do one or two deals a year. There are also players who have made the real estate game their full-time profession and do nothing else. Just as there are an unlimited number of levels of the game such that anyone, whatever his financial position, can participate, so there are infinite possibilities as to one's degree of involvement in the game. You can play one day a week or seven. So long as you don't sacrifice diligence and preparation, there is no required minimum.

In this chapter I have attempted to outline some of the elements of entrepreneurship in order to assist you in analyzing your own tendencies and thereby help you make a decision as to the extent of the commitment to the real estate game with which you are comfortable.

The Fear of Failure

In the Introduction to this book I discussed risk and suggested that you consider your own particular ability to deal with it. There I was talking about your ability to deal with the prospect of the loss of money. When I discuss failure, I am talking about something broader.

Failure is the entire bag of consequences of an unsuccessful deal. The possible loss of money (which hopefully you have defined and limited) is certainly part of it. But also a big part of failure is how you handle both your own and others' feelings about your public flop. Therefore, you must consider your ability to deal with the omnipresent possibility that you might fail in front of everyone.[2] How do you handle the fear that others will think poorly of you? How do you handle the fear that your own self-image will be shaken if your deal is unsuccessful?

The point is that all of us fear failure not only in dollar terms but also (consciously or unconsciously) in terms of the prospect of lost prestige and peer respect as well as damaged self-confidence. How a person deals with this fear is important in analyzing that person's entrepreneurial makeup.

I believe that most natural entrepreneurs don't give one hoot what other people might think about their business failures. First, these entrepreneurs have tremendous self-confidence in their ideas and ability to carry them off and may consider failure an outlandish proposition. Second, their self-image is so secure that they don't fear other people's disapproval because they simply don't care what other people think. If they fail, so what. Not all of us are this "together." You must consider your own particular ability to deal with the possibility of failure.

How will you handle this fear while engaged in entrepreneurial activity? As mentioned, some people have no fear of failure because the possibility *seems* so remote or the by-products of failure (loss of money, respect) really don't bother them. Some people feel the fear of failure very strongly, yet are able to use it to their advantage—because they so hate to fail, they force themselves to succeed.[3] They master fear rather than being mastered by it. Some people feel the fear very strongly and are able to deal with it but only in brief and limited doses. These people need the reassurance of positive feedback from their nonentrepreneurial professions and thus cannot play the game full time. Finally, some people are intimidated by the fear that they function poorly when engaged in entrepreneurial-type activities. These people need to question whether they should play the real estate game at all.

There is no right or wrong in dealing with the fear of failure. The point is to analyze your own makeup and decide the extent to which you are psychologically prepared to play the game.

It is Better to Have Tried and Failed Than Never to Have Tried at All

Many of the entrepreneurs I know are more afraid of inaction than of failure. For one reason or another, they operate under the very strong impulse that never trying is worse than trying and failing. These people are driven to be entrepreneurs. They would consider themselves failures if they didn't "take their best shot." Some of these people feel destined to do great things. Others are deathly afraid of being ordinary.

The Organization Man

Some people don't do well in a structured environment such as a large corporation. Others hate the freedom of total entrepreneurship which forces a person to discipline himself as to work habits and schedules.

Most entrepreneurs find the structure and bureaucracy of a large organization stifling. They neither can nor desire to function well within this type of environment.

Most entrepreneurs are not well equipped to succeed at the corporate game. They are usually too independent to play office politics. Most are probably far too impatient to work their way up the corporate ladder. Many do not have good managerial skills, being far more concerned with creativity and the initial implementation of their ideas. In turn, those who succeed in the corporate world would not necessarily be successful entrepreneurs.

Control of Your Destiny

Most entrepreneurs are strongly motivated to control their own destiny. They would much rather live or die on their own effort than be a small part of a very successful whole.

As one person in a large organization, it is sometimes very difficult to see or feel the direct results of your effort. As part of a team, each person contributes toward the company objective. And the connection between your particular input and the end result can often be very attenuated.

The entrepreneur is generally out there on his own. The results of his effort are both very direct and very visible. This connection between effort and result is very important to the entrepreneur—who both needs and wants the direct and immediate feedback.

Similarly, as money is the barometer of success, the entrepreneur wants the ability to earn dollars commensurate with his effort. If he does a spectacular job—be it over time or on just one deal—he wants the monetary benefit of that effort. He doesn't want to wait for bonuses and raises in a situation where the financial reward is just too far removed from the effort.

The flip side of the input/reward connection is security. If you earn only as your deals succeed or fail, you'd better be right as there is no organization to carry you through the tough times. As part of a large company, you generally earn your salary every week, week after week, and you are neither judged nor paid based on your week-to-week performance. There is a real security knowing that your paycheck will be there every week.[4]

Some people are very strongly motivated by the financial security of working for a large company. Others couldn't care less. You should analyze yourself in this regard.

The Creativity Quotient

Entrepreneurship is a form of self-expression. It is the means through which an individual can translate his ideas into tangible applications or products. Entrepreneurship fosters creativity in that it provides a direct opportunity for conversion of concept to reality.

Creativity can be difficult in a large organization. Be it bureaucracy, tradition, organizational structure or just plain resistance to change, the expression and implementation of one's ideas in the corporate environment is restricted.

Creativity is a very powerful force. It has fostered tremendous changes in our society in just a few years—video games, MTV, artificial hearts, zap mail, robotics—none of these existed in the seventies. What does the second half of the eighties hold for us? To a large extent the answer will come from the entrepreneurs—people motivated to create and implement.

The real estate game is an excellent arena for creative expression. As was discussed in Chapter 1, one of the ways to achieve great and immediate success in the real estate game is to be at the cutting edge of new real estate ideas and applications.

Not only is there a lot of room for new ideas in the real estate game, but real estate itself presents a unique opportunity for creativity, in part because it is so tangible. Real estate can be seen and touched. It is physical. It is there. It is a very visible medium for self-expression. The Trump Tower tells you something about Donald Trump. Your projects can be a statement about you and your ideas.

Most people would agree that there is something very satisfying about the creative process: turning ideas into reality. The pleasure is usually heightened when the reality is a successful, financially rewarding business venture or real estate deal.

The Fun Factor

For many of the reasons already discussed, some people find day-to-day business within an organization just plain boring. The security may be nice, but the bureaucracy, the politics, the repetition, the disconnection between input and reward, the limits on creativity and change, the restrictions on personal expression, the ceiling on income—these and other factors can cut down on one's day-to-day fun in a large organization.

Although I have no empirical data, I submit that entrepreneurs are far from bored with their business lives and, in fact, most are having a heck of a good time. Nothing gets the heart pumping like having to meet payroll or receiving a big check. Getting up every morning with several challenges in front of you is anything but boring. And the day-to-day meeting of these challenges—when it has such a direct and personal connection to your life—can be quite stimulating. Finally, when the day comes when your accomplishments begin to meet your objectives, the satisfaction can be incomparable.

I don't mean to suggest that you have to be engaged in entrepreneurial activity in order to have fun at your job. I do believe, however, that the great majority of entrepreneurs really enjoy what they are doing.[5] They are very lucky in that their "work" is also what they choose to do with their lives—they just happen to be getting paid for it.

How does the fun factor relate to you? Might an entrepreneurial venture—even on a very limited basis—be exciting? Might you find the effort itself stimulating and thereby enjoyable? Are you up to trying something new?[6] If your answers indicate a new challenge might be fun, I respectfully suggest the real estate game. As mentioned, the real estate game holds not only a lot of opportunity to make money, but also the chance to really enjoy what you're doing. This fact probably explains why many real estate players—who have long since become financially independent—are still actively playing the game.

Self-Confidence: Taking the First Step

There are people with tremendous self-confidence who believe they can accomplish anything that they put their mind to. Many entrepreneurs possess this quality and are successful in part due to the force of their personality. They believe that they will succeed; they will accept nothing but success. Ergo, they succeed. This trait is not, however, essential to success in the real estate game.

Self-confidence in anything comes with familiarity. None of us were confident the first time we tried to ride a two-wheel bicycle. Soon, however, we developed unthinking confidence in our bicycling ability and most of us many years later will still jump right on a bicycle without a second thought. The analogy is relevant to the real estate game.

At first all the terms and concepts seem very strange. And, what's worse, everybody seems to understand them but you. How can you ever be successful at this game?

Like anything else, the first step is always the hardest.[7] True, the first time you talk with a broker or look at a deal you may stumble a bit and, at worst, look a little silly. But familiarity comes quickly, and with familiarity comes self-confidence. Soon you will realize that success at the real estate game does not require extraordinary knowledge or talent.

The point is that anything new requires a first step. And there's no better way to learn than by doing. Yes, there's risk involved and therefore you can lose money. But so can you lose by doing nothing—you can lose the chance to greatly improve your financial well-being.

While you must, of course, do your homework before entering the game, you must also realize that not every issue can be answered or quantified in advance. If you try to reduce the real estate game to an exact science, you will never do that first deal. Don't fall prey to "analysis paralysis"—a condition of trying to consider and plan for every conceivable eventuality such that you end up doing nothing.

At some point you just have to take the plunge—not capriciously or irresponsibly—but after a reasonable amount of preparation. You should expect some unpredicted twists and turns. But twists and turns can be dealt with as they appear.

Once your confidence builds, you will be capable of attempting bigger and more complicated deals. And you will realize in hindsight that your initial anxiety, while understandable, was in part unfounded. Finally, it is hoped that you will also conclude that taking the first step was one of the best decisions of your life.

Ethics

Some people have the impression that people active in the real estate game are unethical wheeler-dealers. Some are. But, in my opinion, most are not. Moreover, I am quite convinced that you do not have to compromise your personal ethics in order to be successful at the game. One hundred percent ethical conduct and, unlimited success in the game are perfectly compatible.

I do not believe that one person can preach ethics to another. Each of us must conduct our business and personal lives as we think right. But I do suggest that unethical behavior in the real estate game is not in your best long-term interest.

As a real estate player, you are often selling *yourself*—to a prospective investor, tenant or lender; to a seller whom you ask to take back financing; to a zoning board; and so on. You will learn very soon after your entry into the game that a good reputation is absolutely critical. In my opinion, a good reputation is as important to success in the real estate game as knowledge, or experience, or even funding. I respectfully suggest that you therefore work very hard to develop and maintain a reputation for integrity.

Notes to Chapter 10

1.   "**Entrepreneur:** one who organizes, manages, and assumes the risk of a business or enterprise." *Websters Ninth New Collegiate Dictionary* (1983).
2.   Working in a large organization for the most part shelters your performance from public scrutiny.
3.   "No matter how grim the circumstances, there are certain people who cannot permit themselves to fail. Successful

entrepreneurs and athletes have this unique ability." A. David Silver, *The Entrepreneurial Life* (New York: John Wiley & Sons, 1983).

4. There are also questions about long-term security in a large company both for blue- and white-collar positions. If the company has a bad year (even if due to no fault of yours), if you fall out of favor with the powers that be, etc., you may find yourself looking for a new job. The entrepreneur, on the other hand, once having established his own enterprise, does not have to worry about someone deciding to fire or replace him.

5. "Entrepreneurs are happy people, probably because their involvement in everything they do is intense, complete, and built around confidence. Even though their days are filled with people saying 'no' and 'you can't do that,' entrepreneurs keep smiling. They do not become exhausted by anxiety; rather they get tired from working hard at what they love." *The Entrepreneurial Life*, 1983.

6. Remember, none of this necessarily requires leaving your present job—the real estate game can be played within a discrete time commitment.

7. "The journey of one thousand miles begins with the first step."

11

Concluding Thoughts on the Game

I think it's a great game, with dual opportunities for financial reward and personal enjoyment. I won't pretend that success will come easily. But, in my opinion, your effort will be justly rewarded—financial independence the trophy to those successful at the game.

For those of you ready to enter the game I've tried to identify in the following list 10 important suggestions for success in the game. These "Keys" express my opinions. You may wish to talk with other players and read other books. But, as there is always more to learn, at some point (say, two to three months) I recommend that you begin to play, for the best way to learn is by doing.

For thousands of people the real estate game has been a tremendous source of personal and financial satisfaction. Many of them entered the game with little or no money and less knowledge than you have after reading this book. Few of them have looked back. Here's hoping that your decision to enter the game will be one of the best you've ever made.

Ten Keys to Success at the Real Estate Game

1.   PERSEVERE: nothing good comes easy. Determination is more likely to yield success than any other single factor.

2.   IGNORE THE "DOOMSAYERS": for every great idea there are many people who say it won't work and they always have very "good" reasons. Give reasonable consideration to the downside of a deal but have confidence in and act on your own analysis and instincts.

3.   THERE ARE NO SHORT CUTS TO DILIGENCE: prior to going forward on a deal, do your homework. Don't be caught short by facts you could have identified but just missed.

4.   DON'T BE VICTIM TO "ANALYSIS PARALYSIS": every deal will have twists and turns that you didn't think of. Be confident of your ability to handle problems as they arise.

5.   LET THE CREATIVE JUICES FLOW: the real estate game is a great forum for creativity. For example, today there are thousands of industrial buildings available for sale for "a song." The player who comes up with creative uses for this type of real estate will be very successful.

6.   BUILD RELATIONSHIPS: good relationships with the bankers, brokers and lawyers in your community are critical to success.

7.   DON'T FORGET THE "DONE DEALS": too many players lose interest in a deal once it's closed and leased. Remember, these projects are not only present or future "money machines," they are also an expression of *you*. Watch over these properties and they will return not just dollars but also invaluable advertising and promotion of your abilities.

8.   KEEP UP WITH THE TIMES: one of the reasons that the real estate game holds so much opportunity is that the real estate world immediately reacts to changes in our society. Demographic and life-style patterns are changing radically and the result is that new ideas (the cutting edge) can yield huge real estate profits, meaning great opportunity for the ambitious player.

9.   ENJOY YOURSELF: if the game becomes drudgery, get out! Success comes from enjoying what you're doing. The real estate game requires your attention and energy, which you'll invest only if you love the effort.

10. INTEGRITY IS CRITICAL: there are times when every game player is faced with difficult ethical decisions. Without attempting to preach right and wrong, I maintain that a reputation for honor and integrity is absolutely essential to long-term success at the game.

INDEX